MEASURE
of a
LEADER

MEASURE
of a
LEADER

An Actionable Formula for
LEGENDARY LEADERSHIP

AUBREY C. DANIELS

JAMES E. DANIELS

Performance Management Publications (PMP)
3353 Peachtree Road NE, Suite 920
Atlanta, GA 30326
1.800.223.6191

Performance Management Publications (PMP)

3353 Peachtree Road NE, Suite 920

Atlanta, GA 30326

1.800.223.6191

International Standard Book Number: 0-937100-11-0

Printed in the United States of America

10   09   08   07   06   05

Cover and text design by Lisa Smith

PMP books are available at special discounts for bulk purchases by corporations, institutions, and other organizations. For more information, please call 678.904.6140, extension 131, or e-mail lglass@aubreydaniels.com.

ADDITIONAL PRAISE FOR MEASURE *of a* LEADER

Measure of a Leader **is the** *definitive book on leadership. It captures both the essence and the essentials that all leaders need to know and apply to get results from their people. Thoughtful and thought-provoking, this book is packed with interesting anecdotes and useful insights that can be readily applied in any organizational setting.* **Measure of a Leader** *is destined to become an instant classic— a ready resource for any manager or leader who is serious about success.*

Bob Nelson, Ph.D., best-selling author,
***1001 Ways to Reward Employees* and**
The 1001 Rewards & Recognition Fieldbook

Measure of a Leader *does a fantastic job of demystifying leadership as a function of personality and historical impact. As the book points out, leadership can be learned.* **Measure of a Leader** *provides a framework for the development, practice, and measurement of leadership skills simply by tuning in to the behavior of followers. A provocative "how-to" book for those who want to avoid following in Napoleon's footsteps!*

Richard S. Gold
Senior Vice President, Retail Banking
M&T Bank

Measure of a Leader inspires action for deliberate and focused changes in an organization. The links between managers and leaders, leaders and followers, and behavior and consequences become more evident as the measurement tools provided are applied and implemented. I found myself compelled to action!

Wendy M. Tapp
President
LTI Atlanta
Tapps, Inc.

If you're serious about improving your individual skills as a leader, the principles in this book provide you with specific, tangible actions to execute (as well as the behavioral science behind them). This is not a framework for intellectual pondering or pontificating. It's a guide for taking personal steps to improve your performance as a leader.

Jeff Sims
Vice President
Dollar General

ACKNOWLEDGMENTS

Since this book has been 30 years in the making, the list of people to whom we are indebted is extensive. In fact, it is impossible to acknowledge all of them so we will mention the most memorable contributions here.

First, without the contributions of the science of Behavior Analysis, we would not have the methodological underpinnings that give this work its unique perspective. We could not ignore B. F. Skinner, Ogden Lindsley, and Jack Michaels. We have been influenced by the works of so many researchers and contributors that we only mention those with whom we have worked closely: Jon Bailey, Beth Sulzer-Azaroff, Alyce Dickinson, Richard Herrnstein, Thomas Mawhinney, and Theodore Ayllon. We have been particularly inspired by the work of the Morningside Academy staff and their leadership, Kent Johnson and Joe Layng.

Next, are our clients who have tested and perfected the tools and techniques suggested by behavior analytic research. These leaders have taught us much about what worked and what did not. From them we learned the role of meta-contingencies, or how the organization's culture impacted individual behavior for better or for worse. Again, we mention only a few, but these were our most memorable teachers: Paul Broyhill of Broyhill Furniture Industries, Roger Milliken of Milliken, Inc., Will Potter of Preston Trucking, Terry Ivany of Marine Atlantic,

John Connolly of the Center for Management Research, Bill Mandy and Philip Pope of Blue Cross and Blue Shield of Alabama, Jeff Sims of Dollar General, Russell Justice of Tennessee Eastman Company, Neil Biteler of GTE, Jim Horn of Xerox, Rich Gold of M&T Bank, and John Schueler of ANG Newspapers.

Finally, there are those who helped us capture our knowledge of this subject and publish it. These are people who contributed in various ways, expanding our ability to either explain our ideas or to print them: Darnell Lattal, Tom Spencer, Laura Lee Glass, Julie Terling, David Uhl, Gail Snyder, JoAnne Donner, Anne Palmer, Joe Laipple, Sandy Stewart, Lisa Smith, and Brenda Jernigan. Our interactions with this group have, through the give and take of the publishing process, helped us immensely as we tried to express our ideas clearly and in an interesting fashion. They have also made our own work lives much richer for knowing and working with them.

We are deeply grateful for all of those who have functioned as our teachers during our careers no matter what the subject. Any success we might enjoy is a function of their lessons.

CONTENTS

chapter 1

A NEW MODEL
OF LEADERSHIP

There is measure in all things.

Horace (35 BC)

Leadership is essential to every business undertaking, and yet the failure rate for leaders in America's businesses is in the staggering range of 50-60% (Hogan et al, 1994). While such numbers are alarming, they are not unbelievable to anyone in touch with today's business news. Hardly a day passes without reports of some executive who has been forced to resign or has otherwise been removed from a leadership position. Where else in an organization could we afford or allow such failure rates? How can it be that leadership—a subject that has been studied and written about for hundreds of years and is today the subject of over 16,000 books—still produces such disastrous results?

Certainly part of the problem is that no consensus is available on the definition of leadership. After reading scores of leadership books, readers must ultimately draw their own conclusions about the meaning of leadership because little agreement exists on that subject. Even when authors do agree, the terms of leadership are described so broadly that the reader derives only a general sense of what one must do to become an effective leader. Therefore, the lessons that readers draw from leadership books vary widely based on their own personal experiences, objectives, and prejudices.

Because leadership facts are so difficult to discern, most authors approach the subject inductively. That is, they glean anecdotes from individual histories and present them as universal truths. The leaders they study are usually charismatic individuals who have achieved some level of fame. Since these individuals are often heroic or flamboyant, our fascination over what makes them different from the rest of us becomes the focus. This is a dangerous practice, because frequently the individuals studied are deemed effective *in spite* of some of their more defining characteristics rather than because of them.

Fortune magazine publicized annual listings of the 10 Toughest Bosses. It was an interesting list because so many of these individuals eventually destroyed, rather than built, effective organizations. In some cases, it took years to realize the cumulative impact of this leadership style. Yet when the articles were written, the writers assumed that these individuals were effective leaders. Even today one can find books on leadership based on individuals who have since been discredited. For reasons such as this, an intuitive approach is not a very useful framework for investigating leadership.

A more promising approach to determining the essence of leadership would be to develop a testable hypothesis and then use data to determine whether to validate, reject, or modify it. Then we must gather data that validates or modifies our assumptions. Most leadership writers limit their premises to the success of the leader at his or her particular venture. Our contention is that this approach is too simplistic. It's pretty much like saying that the only thing that counts is the bottom line, even when literally thousands of examples prove that this is not true. When it comes to leadership, how you accomplish success is every bit as important as what you accomplish. Richard Nixon and Kenneth Lay are two prime examples of this basic truth.

Jim Collins, author of the books *Built to Last* (2001) and *Good to Great* (2000), offers one of the better examples of the use of data to formulate his premises. Beginning with a more complete and objective definition of great companies, he examined the leaders of these companies and developed several theories as to the cause of their performance. The next step in this process is to collect data on leader behavior that validates these conclusions.

Unfortunately, like many leadership authors, many organizations use a simplistic view of leadership by only looking at the leader's results. Consider, for example, the tragic story of Charles Dutoit, the Conductor of the Orchestre Symphonique de Montreal, who resigned his position at the peak of his success. The tragedy was that the symphony's board of directors was so satisfied with Dutoit's reputation and successes that they were unwilling to interfere with his management style. He had helped the orchestra achieve an international reputation for the quality of its performances. His musicians, however, reached this level in spite of his "harassment, offensive behavior and complete lack of respect" for them rather than as a result of his leadership style. Instead of helping Mr. Dutoit find a way to create followers, the orchestra's management chose to ignore the union's complaints. The result was a loss for everyone involved and a stain on the reputation of a conductor who would have been better served by a more insightful board (*Le Monde*, 2005). The outcome could have been significantly different had they helped Dutoit change his offending behaviors.

But a premature focus on leadership behavior can just as surely obscure what is really valuable. Managing behavior without knowing why that behavior really matters wastes everyone's time and energy. It also distracts people from focusing on the behaviors that do matter. So how is a person to know which leadership behaviors they should develop? We start by describing the *outcomes* that define leadership.

Producing results is the reason we study leadership in the first place. We want to learn how to replicate famous leaders' successes. Since results can be attained despite a leader's behavior, we contend that the ultimate test of leadership is to be found in how results are achieved via the followers' behavior. True leaders bring out the best in their people, whether that is defined by courage and heroism or by integrity and diligence. Leaders are known both by the successes of their followers and by their followers' conduct, or behavior. Successful people who use ineffective leadership practices are merely lucky. Competence comes when successful outcomes are produced by values-driven, purposeful behaviors.

For the purposes of this book, we contend that the leader's role is to establish the conditions under which all performers will choose to execute the mission, vision, and values of the organization. Here the leader is not so much Pygmalion, the mythical Greek sculptor, but Aphrodite the goddess who turned Pygmalion's statue into Galatea, a living, breathing being. The leader gives *animus* to the organization, not just form.

A New Model of Leadership

We propose a different model to identify effective leaders. Just as we do not look at the moon to determine its importance but rather at its effects, such as on the tides, the earth's crust, the earth's wobble, and the time of rotation, we look at the followers to determine the quality (the effect) of leadership. We are not examining leadership in terms of a person's position in the organization. *We are discussing the effect that any one person has on the behavior of others.* Leadership is a daily activity in every walk of life. In business, we simply have more opportunities for deliberate practice and evaluation in a more controlled setting. Businesses can truly be a school for leaders. For that reason we begin with a simple statement of our premises.

You are a leader only if you have followers. While this seems obvious, its implications are not. It suggests that the focus of any study of leadership should be on the relationship between the leader and the followers, not just on the leader. And to do this effectively, we must examine closely the followers' reaction to the leader. Follower behavior, not leader behavior, defines leadership.

Our model posits four criteria of the followers' behavior that define leadership:

1. Followers deliver discretionary behavior directed toward the leader's goals;

2. Followers make sacrifices for the leader's cause;

3. Followers tend to reinforce or correct others so that they also conform to the leader's teachings and example;

4. Followers set guidelines for their own personal behavior based on their perceived estimate of that which the leader would approve or disapprove.

The first criterion suggests that the most effective leaders are those who get more out of the followers than the followers are required to give. In essence, the individuals donate some of their time and energy to the leader's cause. The second criterion states that the follower is willing to make sacrifices to advance the leader's cause. This implies a commitment to the leader and his cause and is another example of a voluntary choice rather than a forced one.

The third criterion talks about the relationship the followers have with each other as a result of the leader's example. They agree that the leader and his objectives are worthy enough that they will be supportive of, rather than competitive with, one another. And, finally, the fourth criterion is about the followers' relationship with the leader. The follower and the leader respect each other for what each contributes to the cause.

We will have much more to say about these four criteria later as we develop the measures of leadership.

The Difference Between a Leader and a Great Leader

Most of the leaders studied in leadership manuals are charismatic personalities. Unfortunately, this approach leads to the assumption that the secret of leadership is native to the person. However, much of leadership is to be found in context. Would Churchill have been considered a great leader without World War II? Probably not. Yet Churchill did not change his personality so much as did the situation, which called forth different responses from both Churchill and his followers. In a historical sense, we judge the *greatness* of a leader by three factors:

1. *The magnitude of their impact.* Leaders such as Jesus and Mohammed have been judged by the vigor and growth of their message and by the pervasive influence of that message. When others base their life decisions on the example or teachings of a leader, one of the conditions of greatness has been met.

2. *The duration of their impact.* Great leaders produce disciples who extend their message and example well beyond their immediate temporal role. How long the leader remains a significant influence to others is a significant part of the leader's legacy. Leaders such as Jack Welch, former Chairman of General Electric, may be judged as *great* by their contemporaries but leaders' legacies depend on how people in the future recount their stories. Napoleon and Caesar have been studied across the centuries and have been emulated in fields far beyond the military. Only time will tell whether leaders such as President George W. Bush, psychologist B. F. Skinner, or Microsoft's Bill Gates will have had a greater effect on our society.

3. *The number of followers.* The number of people who follow a leader is significant to this distinction. Fame and notoriety are indicators of the numbers of people who have been impacted by the words or example of a leader. Notoriety is a reflection of the immediate impact of the leader's message. Fame, however, is a function of the universality of the leader's message. So the real test is how long a leader's message influences the behavior of a significant number of people.

Greatness as a leader assumes effectiveness. Since greatness is such a fragile designation when we speak of leadership, we will limit ourselves to talking about *effective* leaders in this work. While we may occasionally refer to people that history has denoted as great leaders, our focus is on anyone with the opportunity to lead others in any venture or cause, regardless of its magnitude, duration, or societal impact.

Leaders Are Found Everywhere

The stories of great people tend to blind us to the abundance of leaders. When we eliminate the three factors that determine greatness from the equation, it is possible to see leaders all around us. In every organization, we see individuals who are not in positions of authority but whom others look to for guidance and approval. Hence, many organizations have both a formal organization chart that describes how information and decisions should flow and an informal way to get things done that describes how things actually work. An organization chart is a management tool, not a device that locates leadership.

Such situations highlight the fact that leadership requires no hierarchal position. Joan of Arc was a peasant; Martin Luther was a simple monk; Moses was a refugee from justice; Lenin was a scholar; Jesus was a carpenter; Mohammed was an attendant of caravans; Gandhi was a small businessman, and Martin Luther King was a preacher. A prominent position in a hierarchy simply provides a platform and an arena to exercise leadership skills, but the hierarchal position is not necessary to the practice. Most notable leaders emerge into public consciousness from a position of authority, but this only speaks to the visibility and scope of influence, not to the nature of leadership itself.

It is true that many individuals meet some of the criteria for a great leader but have forfeited their claim to greatness because of their cause and the way they abused the confidence of their followers. Hitler, Stalin, and Osama bin Laden are all examples of how one can adopt all the forms of leadership, but still fail at the substance of the position. The followers of these people were manipulated to sacrifice themselves to a perverted cause. These leaders' pursuit of power and their causes exacted a very high price from their followers, turning them into terrorists and murderers. We will not attempt to discuss these examples but their legacies illustrate the lethal power that the vision of a leader can exert.

The Role of Management in Leadership

The durability of the leader's vision is dependent on the quality of management. The leader does not have to personally provide this management but its absence means that the leader's accomplishments will not endure. Because of this, one role of a leader is to ensure the quality of management. A leader must be involved in management to the extent necessary to ensure that systems and processes are in place that will outlive personalities, so that the leader's legacy survives successive management changes.

In effective organizations, leadership and management are complementary. To some, the differences between management and leadership are nuances, but to a trained observer they are substantial. Both functions must be fulfilled for the organization to thrive. The more explicit one's understanding of the differences, the more effectively one can learn to fill either, or both, roles.

Focus on the Model of Leadership, Not the Leader

One of the challenges for managers is learning how to be leaders. Many mistake the form for the essence. It is normal for people to imitate others who are successful in their chosen field. So a manager will look to prominent, successful leaders as role models. All too often, however, they copy the very behavior that is an impediment to rather than the cause of their model's success. This is certainly the case in sports. Most fans, for example, expect coaches to be disciplinarians. Their examples are people such as Vince Lombardi, Bear Bryant, and Bobby Knight. When a team is losing, the fans tell each other (and if they have a radio program, they tell the coach) that the coach isn't tough enough. When a coach is fired, one of the criteria for the replacement is that he must provide discipline for his players. Yet Bear Bryant, for one, clearly stated that he was not tough and that toughness in dealing with his players was not the secret of his success. His secret of success was getting the players to *want* to give their best (Grier, 2000). All too many overlook this secret of success because they are seduced by what they see, even though what they see is only a small sample of the leader's behavior.

Most of us, at some time in our careers, have worked for a person who was promoted even though he was incompetent. This occurrence is so common it is called *The Peter Principle* (Peter and Hull, 1969), a phrase made popular by the book of the same name published in the 1970s. Yet it is rare for that person to know this about himself. As far as he is concerned, his promotion was merited. The fact is that few managers use a yardstick for success that is more complex than the numbers on the bottom line. True leaders, however, know that the bottom line is only the beginning of the process for determining their impact. Leadership is all about how people react to what we say and do.

When we recognize and measure the effect of our actions, we gain knowledge about what we must change so that we can make a different impact. Our Model of Leadership provides an objective way of correlating leader behavior and organizational effectiveness. Just as looking to the North Star permits a captain to guide his ship into port, observing the behavior of the followers permits leaders to continuously develop their skills.

chapter 2

THE SOURCE OF POWER

I repeat . . . that all power is a trust; that we are accountable for its exercise; that, from the people, and for the people, all springs, and all must exist.

Benjamin Disraeli (1826)

A person who believes that power is "the ability to compel obedience" has stymied his ability to accomplish great things. The more appropriate definition of *power* is the "capability of acting or of producing an effect." It is the effect they have on followers that demonstrates to leaders that they do indeed have the power to accomplish great things.

Leaders derive their power from the network of relationships they develop over time. In business enterprises, this can look like a limited number of relationships that are defined by common interests. The president of a company looks to the relationships formed with the chairman, the board members, and direct reports. At a certain point, it is easy for leaders to believe that their power comes from themselves or from those who empower them, meaning those who put them in their jobs. This would be a mistaken conclusion. Those above us give us authority and responsibility, not power. For leaders, power always comes from the follower.

Politicians are forced to recognize this fact because the electorate gives them authority, responsibility, and power. In organizations these three are frequently separated. A manager can have responsibility but not authority. This is not how it should be but this is usually the reality. A manager can think he has power because he has the ability to hire, fire, or promote. But that is authority, not power. For leaders, *power* is a verb, not a noun. Power is when the leader's efforts are amplified by the organization into a more forceful response than the leader can produce alone.

Power, then, is when the leader acts in such a way that the rest of the organization takes on the responsibility for a coordinated and focused action. The emphasis is on the leader's actions. Words without acts are the equivalent of wishing. Acts without words can be misunderstood. For power to be exercised, both words and deeds must occur that are coordinated to demonstrate how the followers should respond. These words and deeds must be focused in such a way that the benefits of the proposed actions are obvious and imminent, both for business units and for individuals.

The Primacy of Vision

Some of the benefits of achieving the leader's vision may actually reside in the future and be somewhat obscure to the general workforce. The function of the leader is to make those intangible and uncertain outcomes more concrete and pressing. This is how political leaders have convinced people to fight and possibly to die for their country. Spiritual leaders also understand this. Their function is to help the faithful view heaven and hell, not as a concept, but as a fact. For the pious, God's judgment is not a possibility; it is a certainty. These leaders relate everyday actions to milestone markers so that followers can feel their progress and see their objective. In business, leaders must accomplish a similar feat, collapsing time and probabilities so that the consequences of success or failure stir everyone to action now. To this end, many political and some business leaders have adopted the characteristics of the spiritual crusader. They raise the stakes as high as they can to galvanize their constituents to action. They adopt flamboyant mannerisms as a motivational technique. Remember, however, it is the drama, not the dramatics, that makes for good leadership.

Power Resides in the Follower

While the leader exercises power, the source of that power resides with the followers. They choose to extend or withhold the leader's power on an individual basis. Only when the individuals act at the leader's request do we see power being wielded. The failure of many competent people has come because they believe that the flow of power operates in the opposite direction. They see leadership as a command-and-control function. These leaders tell individuals and groups what to do and how to do it. This is an illusion, just as the oasis in the desert is typically only a mirage for the parched traveler.

In a commercial enterprise, we exercise no power over someone who chooses not to work for us. We can exercise no power over someone who withholds discretionary effort. So long as individuals imitate the effort level of their peers, we have no way of forcing them to perform at higher levels. In fact, there are legal as well as moral restraints on our ability to force compliance. And *compliance* is a word that signifies some minimal level of effort rather than a vigorous one. Force, used in leadership, signifies a deficiency that can only be temporarily compensated. Frequent or continued use of force identifies the deficiency as residing in the leader.

If power resides in the follower, then effective leaders must first learn what matters to their followers. Leaders do not impose their ideas on the group. Rather they connect the values, aspirations, or frustrations of the individuals to the leader's own vision. It is senseless to call people to arms when they feel no threat. It is useless to paint a picture of a future that individuals cannot connect to their own requirements and desires. A leader who is out of touch with the needs and goals of the individuals in the group has no appeal and no way to mobilize the group's efforts toward some common objective. Force becomes his only tool.

Functions of a Leader

Leaders say for us those things we want to say and point out the direction that we want to go. Many times we don't recognize our own aspirations until the leader speaks out. Churchill articulated the determination of a nation when he proclaimed, "We shall defend our island, whatever the cost may be . . . we shall never surrender" (Churchill, 1940). Bill Clinton was ridiculed for saying, "I feel your pain," but millions were convinced that he did. And, sensing that he did indeed understand their situation, they followed him in spite of criticism from many sources.

Military leaders who ignore the aspirations of their followers must spend enormous amounts of time and effort simply keeping the troops in combat. Under such conditions, desertions run high and direct conflict with the enemy is avoided. In these situations high levels of activity result in low levels of accomplishment. The energy requirements of the leader increase in direct relationship to the decrease in the commitment of the followers. The opposite is also true. Followers, who identify with the leader's cause, free the leader from supervisory functions so that the leader has more personal resources to apply to the cause.

The single most important leadership function is to create a focus for the group's behavior. As it says in the Bible, "Where there is no vision, the people perish" (Proverbs 29:18). In organizations without this focus, or vision, performance slowly atrophies. Individual groups create their own vision of how things should be, resulting in a multiplicity of goals that are often in conflict with those of others. The resulting loss of harmony either dissipates everyone's energy or increases conflict as each unit pursues its own vision.

The leader who insists that everything is important diminishes the importance of everything. It is the leader's responsibility to clearly distinguish for the followers which activities and goals are important and which are not. Simply increasing the scope of effort reduces a leader's impact. Conversely, tightening the scope clarifies the resource needs and thus facilitates the tasks at hand.

The old expression "Jack of all trades, master of none" is of particular significance to leaders. It says that the more you ask people to do, the less they can do any one task well. The leader's function is to increase the reinforcers for the followers' behaviors that are mission-essential and to reduce the reinforcers available for behaviors that are non-mission-essential. This requires that the leader simplify the requirements for success to a minimum set of actions and that she delivers frequent, positive consequences to those responsible for carrying out the mission.

Once the parameters are set, leaders must stay the course. This does not imply rigidity. The captain of a sailing vessel does not keep the bow pointing in the same direction regardless of the environment and circumstances. To do so is to flounder and to make progress more difficult. Rather, he keeps the orientation constant, always knowing the destination, even when he has to steer in another direction to get there. Leaders are constantly shaping the behavior of their followers, much as the captain trims his sails with a vigilant watch on the compass and on the direction of the wind.

But still, the need to act must spring from the follower, not just the leader. The leader's contribution is two-fold. First, the leader recognizes the commonality of the followers' yearning and articulates it. This must be done in such a way that the follower believes that the leader is genuine in his understanding and in his belief of the importance of the followers' needs. Then, the leader must give a clear and unmistakable call to action. This involves coupling the followers' desires to some specific objective (which probably coincides with the leader's own personal agenda) that produces concrete actions toward its fulfillment. Keep in mind that a leader who stirs the crowd to action but provides no structure to direct that behavior is simply a rabble-rouser. The followers turn into a mob which then either achieves some quick action or which confronts some difficulty (often in a negative manner) and then quickly returns to the daily routine. It is imperative for leaders to ensure that structures are available to support the behaviors they initiate.

In almost all situations these structures are interlocking relationships designed to provide support for the required behaviors. They are designed to keep the performers engaged and encouraged as they do those routine and perhaps repetitive activities that are necessary for success. In any military engagement, for example, only a small percentage of the unit is actually in combat. Without the dependable functioning of the support troops, the soldiers on the front cannot fight the war. The leader who only focuses on those in the foxholes cannot develop the flexibility and responsiveness to exploit any gains his forces achieve.

The workings of this structure are management's responsibility, but its design and efficacy are leadership issues. It is a leader's function to ensure a consistent approach to managing follower behavior. This entails designing a methodology for the management of resources. Since people are the key resource to a leader, this methodology must emphasize the use of the most effective techniques for managing people.

Allowing managers to motivate employees as they see fit introduces a significant amount of variation into the equation of organizational performance. Like Terry Ivany, former CEO of Marine Atlantic advises, "If you feel the way we are trying to manage is unethical, immoral or just a bad way to manage, you will not be happy here because this is the way we are going to run this company." But simply laying out your expectations is not sufficient either. Leaders must examine the methodology of their managers in producing directionally sound performer behavior. Our experience clearly indicates that management methodology is the single biggest contributor to variability in organization outputs. So, leaders must determine if their organization's management methodology is adequate for the task. If managers are to be assessed by a single criterion, it is that of understanding the science of human behavior and applying those principles to their direct reports.

chapter 3
ABOVE & BEYOND:
DISCRETIONARY EFFORT™

The leader, then, not only has to inspire people to make difficult choices
in favor of the vision, but also to inspire them to continue
making that decision over time.

The Authors

Discretionary behavior is defined as "that behavior which a person could do if they choose, but for which they would not be punished if they didn't." It is what we commonly refer to as going above and beyond the call of duty. While you will see some of this behavior in all organizations, the percentage of individuals volunteering discretionary effort is one of the most vital indicators of positive leadership. We all know of people who do more than their peers. This is a form of discretionary behavior. Effective leaders know how to elicit this type of performance from a significant number of individuals such that the general characteristics of the organization are those of energy, initiative, and determination.

Leaders Focus on Discretionary Behavior

Will Potter, former president of Preston Trucking, was an exemplar at eliciting discretionary behavior from his employees. One example of this discretionary behavior was demonstrated by a truck driver who, out of work because of the depressed economy, put on a coat and tie and began making sales calls on potential customers in his community for Preston. He expended this effort completely without management involvement or foreknowledge. Another truck driver, on a day when snow prevented him from operating his company vehicle, used his own four-wheel pickup to complete his deliveries.

Military history is replete with victories won by the initiative and heroic efforts of individuals. While the story told may be about the leaders and their armies, the key to the victories is always to be found in how the individual soldiers fought. Similarly, many political leaders whose names have been entered in the annals of history would have accomplished little without the voluntary contributions of their followers. The old saying about leadership, "Where are they going? I must lead them!" has more than a ring of truth to it. In some cases of follower initiative, the most difficult task of the leader is keeping followers focused rather than keeping them motivated.

In all companies you will find individuals who deliver this extra level of performance. In many companies where overall performance is average, the managers whine, "Why can't everyone be like that?" The outstanding performer becomes the standard of comparison in their eyes. Then, everyone else is judged against that standard. Using outstanding performance to criticize other performers is evidence that the manager is no leader.

In marginal companies you often find managers more interested in conformity than in performance. This happens when they attempt to get everyone to adopt some arbitrary practice rather than studying the relationship between behavior and mission accomplishment. We once worked with a company where a pack builder in a fiber manufacturing plant was performing at a level 20% higher than the rest of the shift. His peers complained that he quit producing each day at least two hours before the end of the shift. His manager reproved him for this behavior and required him to "work the whole shift, just like everyone else." His performance quickly dropped to the same level as everyone else's. Finally, when asked why his performance had fallen, he stated that he had always used the last two hours of his shift preparing for the next day, re-stocking supplies, inspecting his equipment, cleaning, and making other necessary adjustments so that he got a fast quality start each morning. When told by his supervisor to go back to the way he had been working, his performance jumped to almost 25% above the rest of the crew. By initially focusing on the regular procedure and not on specific behavior, this manager risked significant performance losses from this individual.

In excellent companies the exemplary performer becomes not the standard for comparison, but the subject of a root-cause analysis. What is so different for that person? How does his or her behavior differ? Why does it differ? What environmental influences can we identify that can be applied to all performers? Can we enlist the exemplar in the re-design of the work? Since we know from scientific research that behavior is a function of its consequences, we attempt to find the consequences supporting this person's behavior. When answers are found, the organization attempts to create the same conditions for the other performers.

Discretionary behavior is the product of positive reinforcement, never of punishment. Under the conditions of positive reinforcement, when the performer is working to achieve some personal benefit, the behavior can be, and frequently is, long lasting. As long as the benefit is earned and meaningful, the person will keep at the task. Under the conditions of negative reinforcement, the performer may deliver extra effort but the duration and the consistency of that effort will always be suspect. The impulse to escape or to avoid punishment is so powerful when the threat necessary for negative reinforcement is maintained for a long period, that discretionary effort tends to diminish to the point of compliance. You cannot take a snapshot of behavior at any given moment and determine whether it is discretionary or escape-or-avoidance. While both forms of reinforcement can produce extra effort, only positive reinforcement will give an organization the *sustained* characteristics of energy, initiative, and determination.

The best leaders deliver reinforcers to their direct reports but their more pressing concern is to ensure that positive reinforcers are being delivered effectively to all individuals in the organization. Recognizing that reinforcers come from both the task and from management or leadership, leaders must focus on the reinforcement systems. These institutional processes and procedures best ensure that managers are using a management strategy that puts every person's potential first. When workplace activities are intrinsically punishing, the leader must create reinforcers that effectively override the punishment. When this is done in warfare, for example, taking that hill becomes more important to soldiers than the risk of injury or death. For workers in a political campaign, winning the election becomes more important than the flaws they see in their candidate. For performers in an economic enterprise, mission accomplishment becomes more important than the punishers they experience such as lost personal time, problems with suppliers, or conflict with other departments or peers.

Creating discretionary behavior is more difficult for leaders in a hierarchal structure than it is for managers. This is, in part, because the leader must often work through his or her managers. Every layer of management the leader works through increases the complexity of the task. This is because each manager acts as a filter in determining what will be passed on to direct reports. This is not to imply different agendas, competing visions, or willful obstruction, though those factors can also contribute to the problem. Rather, it is simply a matter of the difficulty in understanding and interpreting another person's message. Leaders must find a way to communicate to direct reports and to make sure that the same message reaches all personnel in the organization. This is not an easy task.

Becoming Likeminded

We once worked in a computer manufacturing plant where management had an elaborate goal setting and alignment process. As part of our work in helping them execute their strategy, we had each manager create a plan to drive their top four goals. In many instances, managers exceeded their goals in a very short time. Proud of these accomplishments, we took some examples to the senior executive. His reaction puzzled us, as he barely took notice of results that were producing a significant return on investment.

When asked why these results were not important to him, he complained about the beatings he was getting from his boss about late shipments. Knowing that making shipments on time was one of the four original goals for the plant, we began looking for existing behavior-based plans that supported this outcome. There weren't very many. Shocked by this, we created a focus board to help visualize where management attention was being directed.

We created an organizational chart on a wall large enough to include data on over 100 managers. Next, we color-coded each plan as green if it directly supported one of the four plan goals and red if it supported one of the major goals indirectly or not at all. When we were done, the wall was a sea of red. Upon seeing this, our client noted, "Now I know why I feel like the captain of a supertanker trying to dock my ship with a broken rudder."

We have since repeated this focus board exercise in many companies, and frequently find the same results. This inclusion of non-mission-specific initiatives is caused by the fact that managers deliver consequences based on their own priorities. These priorities frequently differ from those of the organization. A common example is when a manager has three of four objectives that directly support the boss's priorities. The fourth, however, is unique to the manager's position. As a result that manager applies consequences differentially, encouraging more attention to the fourth objective, which dilutes the effort put into the first three. By the time this distortion filters through several layers of management, individual goals and consequences bear only a pale resemblance to the original plan.

As we have pointed out, a leader's first and foremost challenge is to obtain discretionary behavior from managers. Implicit in this, however, is gaining the managers' cooperation in implementing a common methodology for obtaining this same discretionary behavior from all other employees. Then the task is to keep that effort focused on the organization's mission and vision.

Sacrifice

What would possess someone to voluntarily leave family and friends and the safety of home to enlist in an army where the pay is poor, the treatment rough, and the risk of permanent injury or death significant? Millions of Americans did exactly this in both World Wars and are still doing it today. We usually attribute this kind of behavior to intrinsic qualities of the individual. We say that they are patriotic, heroic, adventurous, ambitious, or we give them some other label depending on our point of view. If we admire their behavior, we give them positive attributes such as patriotic, courageous, or determined. If we find their behavior in conflict with our views, we label them in a derogatory manner, such as foolhardy, misguided, impetuous, or stupid. Our label, however, does not begin to really answer the question, "Why would they do that?"

In a more business-oriented environment, most people in our society look at salespersons or telemarketers and say, "I could never do that." When we try to find the answers as to why a salesperson or a telemarketer puts up with high levels of rejection, we once again fall prey to the easy answers and say it's because of the money they earn. Easy answers are usually partial and misleading. The truth is that many people who take these types of jobs leave them within a very short time. The money alone, even in large amounts, is not enough to keep them working at a job that includes repeated, daily rejection.

Effective leaders know that money is only a part of the answer to the question, "Why do people do that?" A soldier who fights for the highest bidder is called a mercenary, but most soldiers are far from mercenary. Organizations that expect to survive in the marketplace require more than the transitory allegiance that chasing the money provides. *The leader's function is to give as many people as possible a cause that transcends their financial involvement.*

A good leader gives people a cause they can believe in. That cause, or vision, doesn't have to be extraordinary. It simply has to be something that explains why the things they do each day matter. It provides to the maximum number of people a way to evaluate the choices they make each day so that their choices benefit the company as well as themselves. That vision energizes them to do just a little bit more than they have to because they see the connection between their efforts and the larger group's success.

Leaders create visions that inspire sacrifice. Sacrifice is not the objective, yet the leader's vision often causes the followers to give up things that are enjoyable in the moment in order to advance some objective of the organization. Wise leaders ensure that these sacrifices are noticed and appreciated individually. If these choices are taken for granted, they will soon disappear.

A leader who allows individuals to sacrifice their personal relationships through long hours or to jeopardize their health or their professional futures ultimately loses the opportunity to lead. The kinds of sacrifice that individuals make, however, do not always have such a heavy cost. A salesperson who, instead of quitting at five o'clock makes one more call, or an equipment operator who stays past the end of a shift to make sure that the oncoming workers get off to a quick start, are making sacrifices. The smoker who foregoes a smoke break to get additional tasks done is also making sacrifices. It is a foolish person who considers these behaviors to be requirements rather than choices.

The tragedy of most mediocre organizations is that the managers are desensitized to the sacrifices their people make. They take for granted the small, daily choices and treat them as if they were inconsequential. When they don't ignore them, they trivialize them. We have seen, for instance, too many organizations with suggestion programs in which employees' ideas are dismissed in such a way that people learn quickly to keep their ideas to themselves.

The leader, then, not only has to inspire people to make difficult choices in favor of the vision, but also to inspire them to continue making that decision over time. If this choice persists long enough, ultimately employees will not think of their extra efforts as sacrifices but as the way we do things here because they will be the beneficiary of the satisfaction and other rewards associated with success of the organization.

How do you get a large group of people to engage in acts that do not provide them with any immediate, positive benefits so that your objectives are met? How do you get them to make these sacrifices? You focus on the consequences of behavior rather than the results, such as improved customer service, increased quality and productivity, and by giving people a way to personalize and relate to the changes you request.

chapter 4

LOYALTY:
IT'S NOT ABOUT
THE LEADER

Discipline is the soul of an army.
It makes small numbers formidable;
procures success to the weak and esteem to all.

George Washington (1759)

Loyalty as used here means the tenacious adherence to the disciplines and practices advanced by the leader in pursuit of the goals and objectives of the organization. For example, though they died in 1939, the Mayo brothers of Mayo Clinic fame still influence decisions in the clinic today. In meetings where difficult decisions are to be made, the question is often asked, "What would Will and Charlie do?" Staff members remind each other that Will and Charlie's guiding philosophy was, "The best interest of the patient is the only interest to be considered."

It is impressive in any organization to have leaders who still have influence even though many years have passed since they left the organization. This phenomenon is not restricted just to the founders or former executives of a company. It can be found at any level within the organization. Front-line employees can be heard to say things like, "If old Bill was still here, he would never put up with that." If employees follow the leader, whether present or absent, and encourage or correct others for their adherence to practices, processes, and codes of conduct put forth by the leader, the organization has reached an ideal state. While some leaders create these followers, many, if not most, do not. How do we create an organization where most leaders do?

It's Not About the Leader

It's easy to think of loyalty in terms of being loyal to a person. Certainly in family settings, that's how we frame the concept. But even in a family setting, loyalty is less about the family members than it is about what they stand for. In any undertaking that requires leadership, loyalty to the individual may be how the venture starts, but it is not how that venture thrives. If the leader cannot transfer personal loyalty to loyalty to his vision, he has failed one of the critical tests of effective leadership.

The tragedy of so many entrepreneurs and executives is that they cannot conceive of the notion that their personal interests and those of the organization might be different. This causes them to blind themselves to flaws and faults, both personal and organizational. They punish differences of opinion and ultimately create loyalty as a one-way street. When they ask for input, all they hear is their own opinions repeated back to them. They expect others to be loyal to them, and they feel betrayed when others take care of their own personal interests first. Loyalty to others, for them, is predicated on obedience from others first. When unquestioning obedience ends, so does their concept of loyalty.

Loyalty is not about the leader. It is about the leader's vision and values. Where loyalty is about the leader, the survivability of the enterprise will always be suspect. Leaders who ignore this are like Louis XV, who is quoted as saying, "Après moi, le deluge!" or "After me, the flood!" He knew that the monarchy could not survive after his departure, but did little, if anything, to prevent its demise. While it is impossible to know what goes on in their heads, many leaders, by their behavior, indicate that they cannot separate their personal fate from that of their organization. Since they will not always be there, they are indifferent to the future of the organization after their tenure at the organization ends. This is most evident when an executive refuses to identify and train a successor.

Building Loyalty

On the other hand, true leaders know that a significant part of their legacy will depend on their cause, not just on their personal attributes. For that reason they take care to articulate their vision and the values that will define their contribution. They strive to inculcate these ideas and ideals in their followers. They transfer some of the followers' loyalty to that which will endure and prove worthy over time.

We know the process for transferring loyalty from one thing to another: it is called *pairing*. By this we mean that, when one thing has positive attributes for an individual, other things of little or of neutral worth become more valuable when presented in tandem with that already valued item. We have all witnessed this phenomenon. We ignore a stranger until he is introduced to us by a friend, at which point the stranger becomes someone of interest to us. This works the other way as well. Things that are feared are sometimes generalized to things that, in and of themselves, have no inherent potential for harm. We have seen, for instance, many individuals who are so afraid of their boss that they will be highly stressed when asked to enter his office, even when the boss is not present.

Leaders create loyalty to their cause by how they value the actions of their followers—actions that demonstrate behavior consistent with the leader's vision and values. The leader uses personal influence to spur the follower to action but then follows through in some concrete way to demonstrate that those actions are valued. This pairing of the leader's approval with the actions directed toward her vision and values gives those activities greater importance in the eyes of the followers. Done often enough, the followers come to value the vision for its own sake. We call this *buy-in*.

Actions Speak Louder than Words

For most people, pairing represents a trap rather than a tool. This is because the default approach to follower behavior is to do nothing when their behavior is what we want and to criticize when it fails to meet our expectations. For leaders who work through others, this has the potential for limiting loyalty rather than promoting it because the leader is paired only with some form of punishment. Individuals who are punished by their manager are more likely to punish their subordinates in turn. People, who are positively reinforced by their manager, are more likely to positively reinforce their direct reports in turn. The leader's behavior really does flow down to the lowest level of the organization.

In an environment where the leader uses punishment as an integral part of his style, it is commonplace for escape-and-avoidance behaviors to flow through the layers of the organization. People at all levels tend to concern themselves with limiting their exposure to punishment, and much like soldiers in a foxhole, they keep their heads down and concern themselves with their own safety. Organizations say that they would like for every manager and supervisor to be a leader. This implies that they should take responsibility for performance and find the most effective way to attack problems. But, we know that in an environment where negative consequences are frequent, that is not the natural response. A negatively managed environment cumulatively decreases loyalty throughout the company.

When the performers learn how the leader deals with failure or some perceived fault, they become defensive and more concerned with avoiding the boss's displeasure than they are with anticipating the needs of the organization or with implementing a determined strategy. As a result, the leader must continually increase his or her expenditure of personal energy just to compensate for this lowered level of performance on the part of the followers. And at this point, many performers are no longer followers but POWs, enduring a forced march toward some distant destination that promises only continued or increased punishment.

In an environment where the leader uses positive reinforcement as a style of working with direct reports, that style is also imitated at all levels of the organization. An interesting and important point is that while managers will absorb some of the punishment they receive, they will actually give more positive reinforcement than they receive (Hinton, 1975). This results in a culture where individuals feel empowered, where they feel committed, or where they form supportive relationships with their peers and managers. In the more tangible aspects of such an organization's culture, you find a higher level of performance, both individually and collectively. Here individuals are actually making the choice to be followers because the leaders have made sure the followers have experienced personal benefits resulting from the success of their units and that of the company. By participating in the reinforcement that comes with success, they connect their actions to department and company achievements, and they perform at levels higher than the organization can reasonably demand but which are freely given for the benefit of the whole enterprise. This is the essence of discretionary behavior and the fundamental building block of loyalty.

The Leader Shows the Way

Loyalty is a habit, not just an act. It grows out of repeated experiences of working at implementing a vision, adhering to values, and finding reinforcement for doing so. All successes have the effect of narrowing the range of responding. This means that behavior that is successful leaves less opportunity for a different response. The more successful I am at one behavior, the less likely I am to try some alternate response. So as individuals find behavior that is successful for them, they tend to repeat it. Whenever the signals of successful behavior are visible to the performer, not only do those individuals tend to repeat the behavior but those who observe that person's success tend to imitate the behavior as well. Over time the organization will acquire common characteristics based on the behaviors that large numbers of individuals find will earn reinforcement. This is the way that loyalty becomes a characteristic of the followers.

But this tendency to imitate successful behavior contains some perils. Without the proper signals, people may imitate non-productive, trivial, or even harmful behaviors. Many parents cringe as they see their children mimic the very traits they are so desperately seeking to change. This same problem exists in organizations. We worked in one location where the plant manager was a workaholic. It was his usual practice to come in early and stay late. Most of his subordinates did the same. However, although the plant manager stayed late to work on substantive matters, his subordinates only marked time. Because much of their work was supervision, when their employees went home, there was little for them to supervise. In fact, they were more likely to be a hindrance to the oncoming shift than they were to accomplish anything. These subordinates developed the form of working hard rather than its substance.

It is the responsibility of leaders to help followers sort out effective behaviors from ineffective ones. All behavior comes at a cost, even those characteristic of loyalty. When we elect to do one thing, by necessity we choose not to do something else. When followers imitate non-value-adding behaviors, they are reducing the opportunity to perform value-adding actions. So, how is the leader to know which behaviors are being imitated?

First, sample behavior at all levels of the organization, looking for both effective and ineffective examples. The behaviors that the leader is concerned with are the ones that a significant number of people choose to do. When a leader sees common practices that produce a benefit to the organization, the leader should celebrate that fact with the performers. This simply means that the leader calls attention to the behaviors and links the behaviors to the benefits they bring to the unit. An effective leader celebrates the ordinary. If you only celebrate extraordinary behavior, by definition this will be a rare event and is unlikely to give people sufficient guidance and motivation for their daily work.

When, as a leader, you find ineffective practices, look first to the system and the process for an explanation. If multiple people engage in ineffective practices, the cause is most likely to be in how their work was engineered. This can be in the way the workflow is structured or how the management of the work is structured. Either way, look first to those systems for an explanation. The most effective remedy is usually to change the consequences for common ineffective practices rather than to punish the performers. If you have a large number of people abusing the sick leave policy, coming to work late, or some other undesirable or unproductive behavior, you can be pretty sure that they are acting rationally, given the system in which they find themselves. The fact that most followers act responsibly does not mean that the individuals involved in undesirable behavior have some character flaw. You have simply designed a system that provided reinforcing consequences for certain problem patterns of behavior.

Second, seek input from your direct reports on how your behavior impacts your followers. We do not seek out negative information about ourselves unless it helps us in some way. Unless the reinforcement from what you learn is greater than the punishment involved in having someone describe your flaws and foibles, you will avoid this act. If you have truly taught your direct reports to be *loyal to the cause,* they will give you the information that you need to be even more effective. If you have taught them to be *loyal to you,* the usual follower will try to avoid hurting or offending you. This, in essence, prevents you from growing as a leader.

When a leader has led an organization for any significant amount of time, that organization becomes a reflection of the leader's behavior. Much like a mirror, that reflection shows only what the leader demonstrates. Often this reflection is a picture of the virtues of the leader. Many times, however, the image is not flattering. While the leader may not recognize this reflection as his or her own, this is merely a perceptual error. You receive what you reinforce, in individuals or groups.

This is why it is so important to analyze unacceptable or chronic poor performance from the perspective of the followers, not just devise new methods of punishment for undesirable performance. Punishing someone for behavior that was created by actions or decisions of the leader inevitably leads to a less loyal workforce. It is certainly not the case that the individual performers are never at fault, but it is important to understand the origins of problem behaviors. Faulty facts or data lead to defective decisions. It is very difficult to change the behavior of individuals in organizations without a methodology that evaluates the efficacy of leadership practices in a practical, empirical fashion.

The Opposite of Loyalty

While we are predisposed to think of the opposite of loyalty as disloyalty, disloyalty is not what leaders should fear most. In fact, many acts that management sees as disloyal are actually expressions of care and concern for the organization's success. The real act that leadership should fear is indifference—indifference to the vision and values that make the organization unique. Yet indifference is also a product of leadership. When the leader is indifferent to how the followers are managed, or to how he treats his direct reports, the followers will reflect that behavior.

One of the signs that performance is being punished is that the performer's behavior becomes less predictable, which is often visible in the ways they seek to avoid further punishment. This reaction is the opposite of the reaction to positive reinforcement, which makes patterns of behavior much more predictable. This same pattern of unpredictable behavior can also be produced by leaders who reinforce based only on results. If salespeople are reinforced based only on sales, for instance, their outcomes frequently become a function of their territory, marketing effectiveness, or other non-salesperson variables. Frequently, the salesperson who gets the largest bonus works less than the person with the least productive territory. While one takes the orders, the other has to hustle simply to gain the attention of clients. While one builds relationships with the customers through golf and dinners, the other knocks on doors, answers objections, demonstrates how to use or sell the product, asks for the order, follows through with customer service, and works strenuously to satisfy the client. Put the salesperson with the bonus in the low producing territory and the sales figures will collapse. Put the salesperson in the low producing territory in the winner's territory and the market share will make significant improvement. Focusing only on results will always produce behavior that erodes the organization over time. Loyalty that is taught only by rewarding success is usually shallow, with its roots reaching only as deep as the leader's pockets.

Resistance to change, the antithesis of leadership, also comes from the leader. This speaks to methodology again. When change exposes individuals to failure and punishment, they resist. When change increases the person's access to reinforcement, they seek it out. Since one of the leader's key functions is to lead change, he must view resistance as a signal that something is wrong with the process being used to achieve desired change rather than simply passing off the resistance to change as a normal characteristic of human behavior. Contrary to common opinion, it is not normal!

When certain behaviors, or patterns of behaviors, get reinforced over time in individuals, the behavior takes on reinforcing properties. This is why some people value being on time, for instance. They begin to see it as a value that they expect or wish others to embrace as well. Consciously, or unconsciously, they begin applying consequences to others who exhibit or fail to exhibit that same behavior. The more individuals get reinforced for that behavior, the greater the collective impact of their individual consequences on those around them. Normally we think of this in terms of peer pressure.

The common understanding of peer pressure is when most people punish some deviation from a group norm. In heavy traffic, for instance, impatient drivers honk at overly cautious motorists. In schools, children taunt peers for a variety of out-of-the-norm behaviors. The United Nations imposes sanctions on countries for the ways the governments of those countries treat their citizens or for the way they treat neighboring countries. Some professional athletes have been criticized, fined, and then ostracized by their teammates for offensive behavior. Peer pressure is designed to obtain compliance. The person is punished until he stops the unacceptable behavior or until he gives the demanded response.

On the other hand, many groups develop norms, or patterns of behavior through positive means that are not in the best long-term interest of the group members. These non-productive or even self-destructive behaviors usually come about as a result of inadvertent peer reinforcement. We occasionally see individuals risk accidents or injury because they are cheered on by their peers. College students engage in drinking contests to see who can be the last person standing. Passengers in cars, especially when the driver is a teenager, can encourage the driver to speed or to perform some risky maneuver. In his book, *Bringing Out the Best in People,* Aubrey describes the scenario at one company in which spectators and fellow roofers cheered one roofer on as he walked on his hands across the pinnacle of a four-story roof. We all see instances in the news every day in which groups in some part of the world are being positively reinforced for destructive behavior. As a result, the groups' members behave in ways that demonstrate loyalty to the groups' practices, as inappropriate as they may be. It is just as possible to create that same tenacious adherence or loyalty to quality, cost, productivity, and personal behavior standards that cause an organization to excel. It is leadership's job to harness these positive forces and connect them to the organization's goals.

Leaders should not be willing to simply let natural selection determine which behaviors the group encourages. Leaders help groups make those determinations. These decisions are simply too important to be left to the collective.

While a leader cannot monitor or manage all behaviors, the leader can ensure that the individuals and groups align their values and behaviors with the vision. A leader does this by making sure that the critical behaviors are reinforced from the many sources available in the organization in the day-to-day conduct of business. Dr. Robert Eisenberger (1992) has shown that people who are positively reinforced over time for extra effort are characterized by persistence at difficult tasks, high self-control, and high levels of integrity. The leader who knows who is engaged in extra effort directed toward the organization's goals and who then makes sure that those people receive effective reinforcement for such effort creates followers who will not only give discretionary effort toward the current goals, but who will thrive on even more challenging goals and objectives in the future. The company that masters this discipline becomes the leader in its field.

chapter 5

LEADERS & MANAGERS: IT TAKES BOTH

No man is good enough to govern another man without that man's consent.

Abraham Lincoln (1864)

Leaders must fill some functions that are very different from those of managers. It is true that some people fill both roles, and there is nothing incompatible with the two functions. For those people who assume management or supervisory positions, the earliest part of their career is all about learning to manage. This involves learning the mechanisms and functions of the organization. A manager, then, is a technician, who helps people, processes, and systems function together efficiently.

Leadership, when most effective, builds on these management skills. The leadership task is to energize the maximum number of performers to pursue the vision in the most effective way. This is where so many downsizing efforts have failed to improve the organization's chances of success. That failure occurs when the leaders mistake efficiency for effectiveness. The pressure of costs overshadows the leader's need to energize the performers around mission accomplishment so that the organization can meet its challenges more effectively. Leadership is most obvious (by its presence or absence) in the face of adversity. This is not to say that the absence of adversity does not require leadership. Leaders devise new and more effective ways of dealing with any new situation while simultaneously maintaining their followers' focus on the company mission. They accomplish this by energizing the performers to exert discretionary effort.

Much has been made of charisma as a characteristic of leadership, but charisma is not a necessary component of leadership. Leadership occurs when the follower grants to another person the authority to deliver consequences. This is why leaders can appear at any level of the organization. As mentioned previously, hierarchal position does not imply leadership. In fact, the *roles* of management and leadership are independent. Let's face it: American industry has produced some spectacular leadership failures over the last few decades, such as Al Dunlap of Sunbeam, Roger Smith of General Motors, and Durk Jager of Procter & Gamble. For the most part, these were high-ranking managers, not leaders. If you cannot or do not positively reinforce others, there is little possibility that you will ever attain true leadership status, even if you become the CEO. Regarding leadership, an impressive title is only the starting point, not the finish line. Followers will gladly grant managers the authority to deliver positive reinforcement, because when followers experience positive results from that delegation, they are willing to cede more authority. Ultimately they will grant a leader the authority to use sanctions and to punish provided that the use of such consequences leads to greater levels of success and personal reinforcement.

A test of leadership is whether followers will remain focused on the mission and vision when no immediate benefits are available to them for doing so or when there are often many immediate negatives involved in the work. The true leader makes the consequences of involvement so valuable that performers ultimately overcome any skepticism they might have about participation. Even among military leaders who are considered great, few are noted for their use of aversive consequences. Clearly they have used aversive consequences but most great leaders are remembered more for their accomplishments and their ability to inspire (make it reinforcing for people to follow) than for their disciplinary methods. Napoleon, for instance, was quoted as saying, "Give me enough ribbon and I will conquer the world." Clearly he was not thinking of discipline or motivation in terms of coercion and punishment. And Norman Schwarzkopf, the U.S. commander of the Desert Storm forces said that he believed the challenge of leadership was "to get people to willingly do that which they ordinarily would not do" (Marx, 2005).

You can also be a good leader and not be a good manager. Examples abound of leaders who inspired large populations to try to surmount massive odds and to persevere in seemingly impossible quests. Yet at the peak of their triumph, their ventures fell apart. Poncho Villa was one such example. He led thousands of Mexican peasants to take up arms against the Mexican Army and, at times, the United States. His victory was transitory, however, because soon after taking power, he lost it and the reforms for which he had fought. Another example was Peter the Hermit, the monk who, during the Middle Ages, led the Children's Crusade to re-capture Jerusalem. He inspired tens of thousands of children and adults from Western Europe to leave home and follow him. Most died of disease or starvation on the journey or were captured and sold into slavery. Few ever returned home and none are known to have reached Jerusalem. A leader? Yes! A manager? No!

It is much easier to teach someone to be a manager than a leader. The principle reason for this is that there are so many more opportunities to practice management than leadership. Yet *effective* leaders are, consciously or unconsciously, practicing leadership skills each day. They note the overlap between management and leadership and accept the opportunities to develop both sets of skills. Leadership is concerned with getting people to want the reinforcers to be found in the behavior asked for; management is concerned with the delivery of reinforcement for the behaviors when they occur. If you can manage consequences contingently, with an emphasis on positive reinforcement, becoming a leader is a matter of technique. When you discover what is reinforcing about those behaviors that are mission-critical, pairing yourself and the organization's objectives with these reinforcers is an easier task.

Learning to lead is a function of deliberate practice. You refine your techniques and skills by observing the followers' responses. While you may pick up some pointers from the stories of others, you cannot simply imitate what they do. *This intentional search for the impact of your actions will set you apart from those who try to replicate the actions of other leaders.* This is certainly the history of organizations that have developed mission, vision, and values statements. Those leaders who followed through to see what impact these instruments had on follower behavior created a more focused, connected effort on the part of their organization. Those who failed to help followers make the right connections saw their efforts fail. Unfortunately, where these efforts at mission, vision, and values failed, these powerful tools turned into static and useless slogans and wall hangings.

In learning leadership there are no eureka moments. Just as the function of the leader is to lead change, what they do to produce the right follower response must also change. Leaders, for example, constantly examine the mission of the organization. Are we doing the right things? Are we structured to achieve the mission in the most effective manner? Are we efficient? They repeatedly re-evaluate their vision. What does the future look like? Why would someone want to be a part of this organization? And, they teach the values that determine acceptable and unacceptable practices in achieving that vision. These issues come from their concerns and not from a committee. When leaders establish themselves as a reinforcer, people try to answer these questions and practice these values because it is seen as the right thing to do. Again, the leader learns from the followers' responses.

In behavioral terms, leadership is all about making mundane behaviors directed at the mission, vision, and values more valuable in the sight of the followers. Since a leader can't provide enough immediate positives to drive the right behaviors for the organization, how does the leader increase the value of the reinforcers the performer experiences in the commission of their duties? In short, how do leaders make it important to each individual to do the right thing?

Leadership is not about driving people to excellence. It is all about getting people to perform beyond the point where punishment or extinction would have dictated that they quit or find some alternate choice. Those who use punishment freely misunderstand both leadership and management. Faced with the choice between the devil and the deep blue sea, or between the punishment from the boss and the punishment intrinsic in the behavior, people become very clever in finding ways to minimize their punishment. The leader gives people a way to experience positive reinforcement for making choices that might otherwise produce punishers.

If the leadership of an organization tries to teach values through threats and sanctions, they will eventually end up squabbling about the definition of their stated values. For instance, in one company where the stated value is integrity, individuals are expected to report to their supervisor when they make a mistake, whether or not that error caused harm. If the mistake caused damage, their self-report could lead to their dismissal. Failing to report the mistake can also lead to dismissal. This balance of punishment is expected to keep the individuals honest. However, the result is that self-reporting is a wink and a nudge situation. Each unit deals with the regulation according to the manager's personal criteria rather than by following corporate guidelines. Integrity, in that case, has become a matter of local definition rather than a common standard. In another company, a manager told us that his vice president was a fan of G. E.'s former CEO Jack Welch and believed in the validity of his dictum to "fire the bottom 10%." The vice president's version of this process was to give 10% of the employees a performance rating of 1. If an employee received a 1 rating two years in a row, that employee was terminated. The manager relating this saga told us that he had 30 employees, which meant that he was forced to give three of them a 1 rating even if they were good performers. As he related his dilemma he said that he had a high performing group and that it was extremely difficult determining which three should get the 1 and much more difficult to inform those people of the rating. We are sure you can figure out how he solved his problem. He simply passed the 1 rating around so that no one received that rating for two years in a row. Of course, this creates a larger problem for the organization. The unreasonable policy has caused a manager to be dishonest, to the employees and to the organization. The vice president thinks the policy is working because he only sees the result of 10% of the workforce getting a 1 rating so he sees no need to change it. Yet this is a demotivating policy for the managers, for those who get the poor rating and for those who don't get it. This vice president is neither a leader, nor a good manager.

Other choices are available. At West Point, for example, the official Honor Code specifies that, "A cadet will neither lie, cheat, nor steal. Neither will he permit others to do so." The leadership makes honor such a value that cadets, when faced with the choice between duty and honor on the one hand, and loyalty to peers and friends on the other, will choose honor and duty. This commonly understood definition of *honor* is uniformly enforced by the cadets rather than from the command structure.

Leadership and Management—The Different Roles

Leadership and management can complement each other quite well, but the two roles demand a different focus. The five key areas where this different focus is most apparent are as follows.

#1 CHANGE VERSUS STABILITY

Leadership's primary focus is that of creating change. In many situations this means bringing order out of chaos. It could just as well mean destabilizing complacency. The leadership effort is to change *is* to *should be*. That is why one of the outstanding characteristics of effective leadership is creativity. New challenges frequently require unusual responses. Market leaders talk about discovering customer needs before the customer does. One of the best examples of this is Steve Jobs of

Apple Computer. Rather than continuing to focus on building market share in computers, where he held less than a 5% share, he recognized a new, related market and focused there instead. Seeing that computers gave listeners more options, and that music lovers wanted access to their music wherever they were, he recognized that he could capture the lead in portable music with his iPods and iTunes. Rather than continually focusing inward on the organization, he focused on the changing desires of the customer for his direction and vision.

Management, on the other hand, is primarily concerned with stability. Once the change has been implemented, how do you make it work the way it was designed to work? This difference is similar to the difference between planning strategy and executing strategy. Managers focus on creating effective habits which will make the new process more productive. The intent is to constantly refine the process, the product, or the habits that optimize resource utilization. While it may take leadership to introduce an initiative like Six Sigma to an organization, such a process change requires management to make it produce to its potential.

#2 External Versus Internal Focus

Leadership focuses on the environment that is external to the organization. This includes the potential marketplace, the customer base, regulators, societal concerns, and other factors that will impact the future of the enterprise. This is where the vision comes from and it requires a big-picture approach to what the organization does and the impact that it has. This external focus is only of value, however, when the leader can translate the new requirements into internal, focused action.

Management takes an internal focus on the activities needed to move the organization in the leader's new direction. The emphasis is on the resources, processes, and the behaviors needed to accomplish this. Where leaders focus on the interactions between the products or services and the consumer, the manager focuses on the interactions between the processes and the employees to produce the product or service. That is why managers use measures such as productivity, budget, defects, and waste. Their focus is on the details of how the product or service is produced and delivered.

#3 EFFECTIVENESS AND EFFICIENCY

Effectiveness is one of the hallmarks of leadership. The question for leaders is always, "What is the best thing to do?" While leaders consider the efficient use of resources, they also know that effectiveness is the more important consideration. General Ulysses Grant successfully concluded the American Civil War because he recognized that a war of attrition was more costly to the Confederacy than to the Union. Where his predecessors had been concerned with the efficient use of their forces, Grant chose to be more effective. He was not callous to the injury and suffering of his forces but he knew that persistent offensive action was the right strategy. When President Kennedy was asked the question, "Why the moon?" he responded as follows:

> We choose to go to the moon . . . because [these goals] are hard, because that goal will serve to organize and measure the best of our energies and skills, because that challenge is one that we are willing to accept, one we are unwilling to postpone, and one which we intend to win . . . (Kennedy, 1962).

Efficiency is the hallmark of a good manager; taking on the right challenges is the mark of a good leader. Resource utilization is one of a manager's highest obligations. While they, too, ask if this is the right thing to do, their emphasis is typically on correctly doing the tasks that they are directed to do. Can the product or service be produced faster, cheaper, and better with less waste? A manager's priority is to conserve resources rather than to expend them. Toyota's management has demonstrated to the world the worth of utilizing resources wisely. Their *kaizen* approach and the Toyota Way are imitated by thousands of companies around the globe. Their efficiency has given them a significant competitive edge in their industry.

#4 FUTURE OR NEAR TERM

Leadership is oriented to the future and to the unknown. One of its functions is to help the followers overcome their uncertainty over the risks inherent in change and show them how their present effort will produce future benefits that are worth the struggle. Without faith in the future, our daily efforts become meaningless and more burdensome. Routine activities become drudgery. Leadership actualizes visions of the future to give meaning to daily tasks and routines.

Today's tasks are the purview of a manager. Here the focus is on today but with a backward glance at yesterday. That is why their performance indicators are most often short term, showing a comparison of month over month or year over year. Consistent with the focus on improvement, managers are constantly trying to improve over past performances. Certainly, managers look to the future, but they do so to avoid ruining today's performance by surprises, shortages, or other disruptions.

#5 CREATING VERSUS DELIVERING REINFORCERS

The larger the following, the more leaders are forced to invest in creating reinforcing systems rather than directly reinforcing followers. Because they cannot effectively reinforce successfully as many individuals as necessary for success, they must focus on actions which make the reinforcers in the activities more valuable. President Kennedy's call for Peace Corps volunteers is an example. Individuals had for many years joined the Peace Corps and traveled to impoverished countries to help people in those countries live better lives. When President Kennedy called for more Peace Corps volunteers, however, their numbers grew by leaps and bounds. People were asked to sacrifice years of their lives, to forgo significant sums of money they could have earned at home, and to put their health and safety at risk as part of the bargain. Despite those daunting contingencies, Kennedy ennobled the work such that thousands voluntarily made the choice to participate.

While managers also may have large numbers of employees or direct reports, their focus should be on reinforcing individuals for their behavior. The reason for this is strictly functional. The only way to stabilize behavior is through reinforcement. Punishment increases the variability of human behavior and makes it less predictable. Reinforcement makes behavior more predictable and therefore more valuable. Once the leader has ennobled the work, the manager must still strive to keep that sentiment alive once the individual has met the daily reality of hard work and repetition. The best Peace Corps country directors retained large numbers of volunteers for multiple terms of service by frequently reaffirming the individual's contributions to the cause.

Leaders and managers alike are essential to the effective functioning of organizations. Ideally every manager would also be a leader and every leader would be an effective manager. Most organizations, however, structure the environment to prompt management over leadership. Managers' measures, their lack of emphasis on vision and values, and their reward structure drive daily activity on the part of all senior leaders to short-term results and toward efficiency over effectiveness. In addition, a lack of knowledge of follower behavior leads managers to make common sense errors which often suck them into a sandpit of firefighting and reactivity. Leaders are only free to be successful leaders when managers fulfill their management functions faithfully and effectively as well.

chapter 6

IT'S ALL ABOUT BEHAVIOR

When you really see behavior, you see possibilities.
The Authors

There can scarcely be anything more familiar than human behavior. We are always in the presence of at least one behaving person. Nor can there be anything more important, whether it is our own behavior or that of those whom we see every day or who are responsible for what is happening in the world at large. Nevertheless, it is certainly not the thing we understand best. Granted that it is possibly the most difficult subject ever submitted to scientific analysis, it is still puzzling that so little has been done with the instruments and methods that have been so productive in the other sciences. Perhaps what is wrong is that behavior has seldom been thought of as a subject matter in its own right, but rather has been viewed as the mere expression or symptom of more important happenings inside the behaving person (Skinner, 1987).

Although this was written by Dr. B. F. Skinner in 1987, organizations have scarcely changed the way they manage since that time. Books written on leadership today rarely refer to the scientific literature on behavior. Oddly enough, MBA students are not taught about behavior as it relates to management, and most organizations are still managed with only a common sense understanding of behavior, even though behavior is at the heart of every accomplishment from meeting deadlines to making a profit and increasing the stock price.

Starting Point

Leadership is all about behavior. Only two sources of behavior exist in organizations: the behavior of the leader and the behavior of the followers. We speak of leading people but to be precise we should speak of leading their behavior. If we are to be most effective as leaders, we must understand behavior in a precise way. This means applying scientific methodology to the subject of leadership and, thereby, behavior.

If behavior was not lawful, then what one does today would have no bearing on what one does tomorrow. Although people usually resist the idea of using science to manage behavior, most people agree that the best predictor of what one will do today is what they did yesterday. No one denies that we are, for the most part, our habits. If we examine our behavior we will see that a large part of what we do is habitual, whether it is driving a car, getting dressed, or using a computer.

The science of behavior can be applied to the subject of leadership just as it can be applied to other sets of behaviors. Understanding leadership from a scientific point of view will enable one to improve one's own leadership skills and teach these skills to others as easily as we acquire other habits.

Behavior is so much a part of our daily environment that we scarcely notice it. It is only when behavioral aberrations can be observed that behavior comes to our attention. Athletes and musicians are probably more familiar with the importance of precise behavior than leaders are because they can tell immediately if they have performed a behavior correctly. A sour note or a missed shot tells the performer at once whether he has completed the behavior required to get the correct result. On the other hand, in business, behavior is often ignored, as the workforce embarks on a quest for results. Since executives and managers rarely see a product being made, sold, or serviced, they are far removed from the critical behaviors that make those processes effective. The emphasis on results, without an understanding of the behavior that creates them, has caused most of the corporate scandals throughout history. While awareness of the importance of behavior at the executive level is increasing in most organizations, the understanding of behavior in the executive suite is far from precise. Executives talk about the proper attitude, commitment, employee involvement, and, more recently, competencies. *Competencies,* like the others terms and phrases, are actually a form of disguised behavior. While a list of competencies may be a step toward describing behavior, at best they represent a group of behaviors that are almost never understood in a precise way and, as such, lead to inefficiency, misunderstandings, and errors in execution.

No longer can an organization survive where the attitude toward business is "I don't care how you do it; just get it done!" This outdated outlook has ended in an increasing number of executives explaining their actions in front of a jury. Chuck Prince, the CEO of CitiGroup, was quoted in *Fortune* (2004) when talking about a scandal in one of CitiGroup's Asian banks, "I never thought that you had to say to people, 'We want to grow aggressively—and don't forget not to break the law.'" He might think you shouldn't have to be this specific, but actually you do. Businesses can no longer accept any less than people who accomplish results in a way that is efficient, effective, legal, moral, and ethical. The behaviors involved in those accomplishments are in many cases not very well-defined. As business processes become more complicated and lawyers continue to have success in making legal and ethical activities of what once were illegal or unethical, employees in some organizations feel that the end justifies the means. Here at the beginning of the twenty-first century, corporate leaders face an increasingly urgent pressure to redefine legal, moral, and ethical behaviors that they once thought were obvious to everyone. At this point in business, defining those behaviors often requires considerable time, at least in the beginning, but it is absolutely worth the effort in the final analysis. While knowing precisely what behavior to do will not guarantee that it will occur, it does allow us to see the behaviors more easily and to deliver effective consequences for the right behaviors, which is the key to effective behavior change.

Success in organizations is defined by results. The normal measures of executive prowess are generally gauged in terms of sales growth, market share, return on investment, profits, and cash flow. Stock analysts and investors evaluate all of these outcomes and many, many more in determining whether or not a company is successful and whether or not it is likely to remain so. This is the proper approach in so far as it goes, because unless an organization produces results, it will eventually go out of business. That certainly is the lesson learned from the dot.com bust of 2000/2001. Because of the necessity of producing results, however, many managers misunderstand the role of data and react incorrectly to data change. Wall Street and many company boards of directors also react incorrectly, with even dire consequences, when they reward their executives lavishly for rising stock values regardless of the executives' management style or methods.

An example of this problematic approach is Bausch & Lomb. From the mid-1990s this large American company reported double-digit growth. The president of the company was rewarded with large bonuses and raises as the company stock gained significantly in value. The president's method for gaining such growth was through a system of tough goals that, if met, earned significant bonuses for his subordinates. Of course, the penalty for failure was also high, with several key executives leaving because they could not hit their targets. The end of the story, unfortunately, was a disaster for the company. An outside investigation revealed that the Bausch & Lomb product was stockpiled in warehouses around the world. Product had been booked as sold in advance of customer orders and was waiting for demand to catch up with supply. Other shipments were being diverted into the gray market where they were competing with the company's authorized distributors. The fall in stock value was significant and preceded the downfall of the president by a very short time (Maremont & Barnathan, 1995).

Results alone do not tell you which activities to reward or punish. Yet managers react to data changes as if those changes reflect performance change. They think that if the numbers go up, the person in charge must have caused it. And, if the numbers go down, the same must hold true. But this is not necessarily so! Bernie Ebbers, Ken Lay, Jeffrey Skilling, and Richard Scrushy were all at one time the darlings of Wall Street. Now they are at the center of scandals and impending criminal prosecutions for allegedly manipulating their companies' stock prices. The lesson here is that without knowledge of behavior, a focus on results can lead one astray. All results are produced by behavior: the behavior can be appropriate or inappropriate, legal or illegal, encouraging or abusive.

Competent performance at all levels of management is a matter of creating results through the correct behaviors. When we track both the behaviors and the results, we gain a much clearer picture of the relationship between our efforts, the efforts of others, and the success or failure of our initiative. While results alone tell you very little about their causes, behaviors linked to results can be very informative. The following anecdote illustrates how focusing only on results can lead to confusion and frustration.

One of my first clients was a textile mill that spun yarn into fabric. The plant manager was a very effective manager and a good student of behavior. After I spent a good deal of time talking about the need for positive reinforcement, he invited me to attend weekly staff reviews where each supervisor and manager presented graphed data on their top-three performance indicators and discussed the results.

The first-shift spinning room supervisor presented his efficiency graph, showing a strong, positive trend. The plant manager asked him about the cause of this trend. The supervisor stated, "Well, you know how it is with spinning. The higher the humidity, the stronger the yarn. The stronger the yarn, the fewer the breaks. The fewer the breaks, the higher the efficiency. We've had high humidity lately."

At this point the plant manager responded by asking, "What else have you got to show me?"

Of course, I was disturbed because I heard no positive reinforcement for this good performance, even though the performance trend was as positive as any I had seen. If that did not earn reinforcement, what would? So, I decided to speak to the plant manager as soon as I could. The first-shift personnel completed their presentations and left but I didn't have time to speak to the plant manager before the second-shift personnel entered the room and began showing their data. The second-shift spinning room supervisor put his efficiency graph up. The production trend spiraled downward in a strong, negative direction—the exact opposite of the first-shift's data.

As before, the plant manager asked this supervisor the cause of the trend. Unbelievably, the supervisor stated, "Well, you know how it is with spinning. The higher the humidity, the stronger the yarn. The stronger the yarn, the more the breaks. The more the breaks, the lower the efficiency. We've had high humidity lately."

At that point, the plant manager cursed and stated, "I'm gonna fire both of you guys and hire a weatherman!"

–Jamie Daniels

What Is Behavior?

Management books are still being written, and are still popular, that refer to the heart as the origin of discretionary behavior. While metaphors can be useful in communicating certain messages, they are rarely prescriptive. To tell someone that he needs to "put his heart and soul into a project" is an unreliable way to solve problems and create accomplishments.

Technically speaking, behavior is any activity of a living creature. Most of the behavior that organizations are concerned about is observable and therefore measurable. If behavior meets these criteria, it can be changed reliably and efficiently. If not, behavior change is hit-or-miss. Thoughts and feelings are behaviors since they can be observed and counted (but only by the owner of those behaviors). An employee's mind, however, is off limits to a manager or leader, as it should be, because internal behavior is as private as the person deems it. It is not necessary to know an employee's thoughts and innermost feelings to manage or lead. However, consider how people most often respond to the mistakes of employees. We assume when someone makes a mistake that it is caused in part by the fact that they did not think. We say such things as, "What were you thinking?" "Don't you ever think?" It turns out that thinking about the mechanics of what you are doing is facilitative only in novice performers. In skilled performers, it is actually disruptive (Beilock et al, 2002).

By definition, behavior is active. To quote Dr. Ogden Lindsley, a pioneer in the field of behavior analysis, "If a dead man can do it perfectly, it won't solve your problem." A dead employee can make no defects, have no accidents, and have no arguments. No productive outcome arises from any of these conditions. The average organization's leadership emphasizes behavior that the organization doesn't want rather than those that the organization does want. Managers track customer service errors, accidents, near misses, defects, and so on. Focusing on reducing errors is almost always inefficient because it takes the focus away from the behavior that is critical to the desired performance.

Inefficient leadership is often the result of holding managers accountable for results that are not under their control. If an outcome is not directly affected by a person's behavior, why would we reward or punish that person for the results? Holding a manager responsible for profit seems like a reasonable accountability, but when profit is determined by something as variable as the exchange rate of the dollar, holding the manager accountable for profit is a waste of time and detrimental to the manager's future performance. It would be more helpful to hold the manager accountable for production, cost, and quality of the products produced.

In some organizations, the human resources department is accountable for absenteeism and personnel turnover. This is misplaced accountability. HR could do many positive things and still not affect those variables. Most people leave employment, not because of the actions of HR, but because of how they are treated every day by their supervisors. Supervisors are the ones who should be held accountable for absenteeism and turnover except for reasons such as employee relocation, employee illness, and other such cases not under the supervisor's control. Another example is the backlog of orders waiting to be processed, maintenance work orders awaiting completion, etc. Many front-line supervisors have been punished for failing to reduce such backlogs when they have actually processed or completed more work than ever, but as the result of increased sales or maintenance requests, the backlog of work to be done remains the same or is actually higher.

Even when convinced that managing behavior is the most important part of their job, many managers still can't see behavior as important. This is because they have managed by results for most of their careers. Managers need to learn the following rule: *you don't lead **by** results; you lead **to** results; and only behavior will get you there.* We have heard it often, "I know I need to recognize good performance, but I just don't see it very often." We have walked the floors of many offices and plants for the express purpose of signaling the leader or manager to comment on some specific behavior of employees. Teaching leaders and managers the ability to move from general descriptions of a problem to specific desired behavior often determines the difference between success and failure.

What Behavior Is Not

It is important to differentiate between behavior and non-behavior. Of course, attitudes are not behaviors; competencies are not behaviors; values are not behaviors; employee involvement and commitment are not behaviors. Yet, each of these concepts is composed of many behaviors. That is why these umbrella concepts are so difficult for many organizations to change or attain. Telling a person that she has a bad attitude is rarely effective in changing the attitude, even when she is told that if she doesn't change she will be fired. She may make changes in the behaviors she perceives as representing a bad attitude, but they may turn out not to be the ones that the critic had in mind. This may seem burdensome or unnecessary, but failure to be specific about how employees, peers, and customers should act has cost organizations untold millions. Many executives and high-level managers have been fired when changing one small behavior could have saved their jobs. Marriages that were on the brink of divorce have been saved by making a change in behavior as small as "Tell her you love her several times a day." The boss who tells an employee, "Keep me posted on the progress of the project," may mean "Tell me every day how things are going." The employee who thinks reporting once a month is sufficient because nothing much is happening, may find himself in trouble before he even gets to his first reporting date. Similarly, asking someone to smile more often may be infinitely more helpful than telling him to change his attitude.

The easiest way to know if you have a specified behavior is to try to count it. If you can't, then what you are concerned with is not a behavior, and solving your problems with any lesser level of analysis will be difficult indeed.

Problem Solving Through Behavioral Observation

Many front-line employees do not think much of upper management's problem-solving abilities. The reason is not that upper managers don't have these skills but the fault is in their lack of researching, acknowledging, and addressing problems by providing the solutions and resources necessary to solve them. Typically, when an employee has a problem with some aspect of work, he tells his supervisor, who, lacking funds or authority to take proper action, tells his manager, who tells his manager until the problem reaches the proper level for resolution. The problem with this process is that often the front-line performer is a poor observer of his own behavior. As such, he puts his own spin on the problem when reporting it to his supervisor and thereby introduces a skewed view of the real problem. This variation is multiplied several times as it moves up the organization's chain. The solution that executives give for the problem may be perfectly reasonable given what they understand the problem to be, but since they do not fully understand the problem that was originally presented, their solution may not even come close to solving the problem or may attempt to solve it in a way that the employee who submitted the problem considers completely unsuitable.

A way to dramatically improve problem solving is simply to ask, when presented with a problem, "Could I *see* that?" or "Show me what you are talking about." Then go look at people in action, better known as behavior. When you look at behavior, some solutions will occur to you that never would have occurred otherwise. A podiatrist, for example, requires you to walk so that he can observe your walking behavior. The podiatrist can then diagnose many problems just by watching you walk for several feet. He will note specific aspects of your walk that only a podiatrist would notice, such as if you walk on your toes or shift one foot inward. The average person watching you walk would not see these particular movements even if you asked them to look. Athletic coaches are much more likely to see specific behavior when trying to change results than are the average leaders or managers.

When we once presented the findings of our behavioral observations in a bank that had major sales issues, the president slapped his forehead and said, "I've been in banking for over 30 years and I consider myself a reasonably intelligent person. Why didn't I see this?" Our response was, "Don't beat yourself up, because for 30 years you were trained to go into a branch and look for results on paper."

In another example, while we were conducting behavioral observations at a faucet manufacturing plant, the production line went down. During this event, our consultant observed an older employee fold his arms, close his eyes, and start napping. Another left the line to talk to a fellow employee. Another pulled out the newspaper and started reading. Another started cleaning and straightening her worktable, began refilling the parts bins, and picked up some litter on the floor. Incredibly, the supervisor saw none of this behavior. The line was down and no work was being done—as he saw it. Because he was focused only on results— the number of faucets produced—he failed to see the positive productive behavior of this employee.

When you really see behavior, you see possibilities. Thomas Gilbert (1996) gives an example in his book, *Human Competence,* by telling a story about two men shooting at targets. One hits the bull's-eye every time and the other misses every time. Just looking at the results, you can imagine how a poor coach might respond. He might question the poorer shooter's talent, his intelligence, or his motivation to learn. He might say things like, "You are not concentrating" or "You need to try harder." The effective coach would ask the poor performer to shoot while he observed his behavior. As in Gilbert's example, the major difference in the two turned out to be that the poor shot closed his eyes as he pulled the trigger. Small behavior changes can often make a big difference in results. Most problems are caused by employees who do small things wrong. When you reduce problems to small behavior changes, most of them are solvable.

Once you know the behavior you want, you have gone a long way toward a solution. If you know the behavior you want, you can measure it and if you can measure it, you can change it. Learning what you want people to do is the most difficult part of any change process. When we know the behaviors that are important to effective leadership and management, the process of changing those behaviors is reliable and effective. Therefore we turn now to the measures of the followers that reflect good leadership.

chapter 7

AN INTRODUCTION TO LEADERSHIP MEASUREMENT

When you can measure what you are speaking about, and express it in numbers,
you know something about it; but when you cannot measure it, when you cannot
express it in numbers, your knowledge is of a meager and unsatisfactory kind:
it may be the beginning of knowledge, but you have scarcely,
in your thoughts, advanced to the stage of science.

William Thompson, Lord Kelvin (1894)

The Proper Use of Measures

Our focus is to develop a testable hypothesis for leadership develop-ment. To that end you will see that we have described the measures of leadership differently than most authors. If we cannot measure loyalty directly, for instance, how do we recast the concept in ways that permit more direct observation and evaluation? This may lead to the usage of different terms but they always relate back to the four criteria of the follower's behavior (described in Chapter 1) that, as closely as possible, define *leadership*.

It is, however, with some trepidation that we suggest various ways for measuring leadership. We see how often people misuse measures to reward or punish others. The best use of measurement is to provide feedback to individuals and to provide people with opportunities for growth. Rewards, and perhaps even punishment, are not inappropriate when used in the context of encouraging or supporting learning. The primary objection to some forms of reward and punishment is that management sometimes inappropriately uses those consequences as a substitute for the real determinants of motivation and behavior change: supportive, interpersonal interactions that use measures to enable the person giving the feedback to best change the behavior of the follower. When measures are changed from tools to assist learning to tools to control behavior, we begin to see the formation of the dark side of the force. This produces a tendency to manage by exception which invites a natural, but deficient, approach to leadership.

The most significant reasons that a leader should measure leadership have to do with the leader's own personal development. With the right measures, leaders can establish a cause-and-effect relationship between their actions and those of their followers. By tending to this relationship, leaders learn with fewer trial-and-error cycles. This, in turn, progresses to a steeper learning curve and a more immediate impact on followers as they perceive and react to the improved leadership skills.

The second reason to measure leadership is that measurement allows one to separate *apparent* effect from *actual* effect. Too many people are already trapped in counterproductive behavior patterns, because they believe in the efficacy of those behaviors. With no way to prove or disprove their impact on the follower, they continue doing inappropriate or ineffective behaviors. This accounts in large part for the 50-60% leadership failure rate we quoted earlier. With measures, leaders discover the true relationship between their actions and the impact those actions have on their own leadership potential.

As you will see from our measures, we are assuming that the leader has a position within some organization hierarchy. While it is true that anyone can be a leader and that leaders appear in all settings, our efforts are to show designated leaders in organizations how to best improve their skills and those of their employees. Thus our measures and our conversation will be directed at those who have some formal responsibility for leading the behavior of others in the organization.

Ways to Measure Leadership

Leadership is already being measured. What's more, these measures are being used to reward or punish individuals in organizations. Since most people are unaware of some critical distinctions concerning human behavior, they use the default method of measurement which is judgment. They frequently compound this error by judging personality while thinking they are measuring leadership behavior.

Too many people confuse personality and behaviors. Personality is usually difficult to change but behaviors are changed every day. Some people claim you can't change other people. This defeatist approach to management and to leadership grows out of this confusion. Changing someone's beliefs and personality is difficult and prone to failure. On the other hand, changing someone's behavior is relatively straightforward and, with the proper understanding of behavior fundamentals, usually successful.

From a leadership perspective, the primary way to change others' behavior so that they become loyal and productive followers is to change one's own behavior first. Given this fact, learning leadership is fundamentally a self-management task. But this task is made immensely more difficult if you think of it in terms of changing your personality, such as becoming more charismatic. Since leadership is defined in terms of the behavior of the followers, the task is to ask, "What do I want my followers to do?" and then "What must I do to produce that behavior?" The measures we propose are simply tools to tell people if their behavior is having the impact that makes an effective leader.

Measurement Versus Intuition

Many people warn against an overreliance on measurement and data. They say that instincts are frequently more reliable than data, especially when it comes to gauging interpersonal responses, such as leadership events. Malcolm Gladwell (2005), the author of *Blink,* warns that too much data can diminish our accuracy in making decisions. You may be surprised that we tend to agree with Gladwell's conclusion. Overanalysis is as big a problem as no analysis, because the more decisions one has to make, the less likely one is to make any decision at all. This is easily seen in the number of call-in customers who, when encountering multiple choices while trying to get customer support, abandon their calls. We do not agree with those who would discard all but the most basic of numbers, however.

A great deal of research tells us that fluent decision making is a function of accurate practice. The more you practice any skill (Gladwell talks about practicing spontaneity for instance), the better you get at it. There is, however, a significant caveat: you must have valid feedback on the accuracy of your execution. Otherwise, practice will only strengthen your bad habits, much as it has done to the average golfer's swing. This is where the role of measurement and feedback comes into play. Decision making can be improved significantly if we can give the decision maker quick, accurate feedback. The longer the delay between the decision and when the effect of that decision is known, the less useful that information is in improving decision making. By the same token, the less precise that feedback is, the less useful it is in improving decision making.

We believe that intuition or instinct is unrecognized experience. It is the same thing that you see in expert performers. These individuals typically have lots of practice in their area of expertise. Someone like Dr. Laura, the radio talk show host, cuts through most of the confusing detail presented by a caller and gets to the crux of the situation quickly. Less practiced individuals sometimes complain that she doesn't listen well and that she is too quick to offer a solution, but experience has taught her which information is relevant and which information is not. Of course, everyone has some type of experience, yet not everyone is an expert. And, even though some people have vast experience, we would never trust their instincts.

We insist on validating so-called instinct and intuition. We have encountered too many situations where one person's intuition was opposite that of another. One of our clients, a Christian book publisher, related the story of firing a worker on the grounds of poor performance. During the interview, the soon-to-be-discharged employee stated, "You can't fire me! The Lord called me to this job."

Leaders who seem to have an instinctive grasp of the choices to make and a natural ability to communicate them effectively are the product of unrecognized practice. While natural-born leaders may exist, such people are as rare as natural-born musicians. How many Mozarts have there been? Most highly skilled performers became masters through practice. Jack Benny, a comedian who played the violin, had it right when he responded to a tourist's question, "How do you get to Carnegie Hall?" His answer was, "Practice, practice, practice!" Leadership skills, and the instincts that accompany them, are acquired in the same way.

Charisma in Leadership

It is not necessary to be charismatic to be a powerful leader. Jim Collins (2001), in his book *Good to Great* states that the characteristic of leaders of great companies is that they are modest and almost self-effacing. Our experience has taught us a similar lesson. For instance, one of our clients, Ralph Archer, a department manager at Kodak, described himself as "not outgoing," yet he created unparalleled levels of excitement among his followers. Managers of other areas commented that walking into his workplace was like walking from cloudy skies and rain into sunshine.

Yet the leaders that seem to interest us most are those we characterize as charismatic. Most of the books on leaders and leadership focus on charismatic personalities even though most successful leaders are not charismatic. An examination of the behavior characteristics of charisma shows that we usually miss the mark in explaining it. As it is usually defined, charisma is so specific to the person and the situation that trying to imitate or replicate it is rarely successful.

The definition of *charisma* in *The Oxford English Dictionary* begins with "the magic . . . ." This term typifies the mystery that surrounds the word. Once again the definition deepens the mystery rather than enlightening it. Who has magic? How do you acquire it? This is a blind alley for the aspirant. By the way they talk about it, writers and charismatic leaders would have us become postulants seeking to embrace and worship the mystery rather than have us become apprentices, learning the behaviors that would help us replicate their successes.

Like leadership, *charisma* is defined by the effect one person has on others. You cannot have charisma without having admirers. We admire people who lead us to successes we would not attempt on our own or who allow us to participate in visions and accomplishments that we would not have imagined without them. *Charisma* is the term we use to describe our reaction to someone who interests us, who energizes us, and who gets us involved in ideas and actions greater than our own.

Learning to be a more effective leader becomes much simpler when we have reliable guides for action. When we attempt to lead others, data on their response can clarify the impact we had and can suggest ways for us to change our actions to produce either different reactions or more of the reactions we have already achieved. Data can accelerate your learning and reduce the time it takes for you to become a natural leader.

chapter 8

MEASURING LEADERS' ACCOMPLISHMENTS

Man emerges . . . ahead of his accomplishments.

John Steinbeck
The Grapes of Wrath (1939)

Traditionally leaders have been measured by the accomplishment—the impact—they have on their particular field of play: politics, sports, business, and so on. In business, this impact is measured in three dimensions.

1. Did they grow the enterprise?

2. Did their enterprise achieve some level of prominence?

3. Did the leader leave a positive legacy?

Did They Grow the Enterprise?

Measuring growth depends on an understanding of the baseline condition of the business when the leader assumes responsibility. Profitability is the *sine qua non* of indices for this purpose in the business arena. It is not the only index, however. Market share, revenue growth, revenue stability, and shareholder return are among the others. Rather than looking at a single number, such as profits, the real measure of growth is more complicated in that it usually contains multiple components. We do not offer a measure in this area as this is best left to shareholders and financial experts.

Did Their Enterprise Achieve Some Level of Prominence?

Some organizational leaders have an outsized influence based on some value other than the profitability of their company. Steve Jobs, CEO of Apple Computer, is an example. Jobs is considered to be an industry leader because of his ability to create and innovate. Apple's products, while owning only a small share of the market, are trendsetters and have created a strong set of followers in the marketplace. Anyone who significantly impacts their marketplace by their products, their efficiency or effectiveness, or by their customer service exhibits significant leadership. This is a measure that is determined by customers and by industry peers.

Did the Leader Leave A Positive Legacy?

This is the measure that is most clearly historical. While we can give an early assessment, this has something of the quality of a prediction to it. A legacy is actually a measure rendered by the leader's successors, not his contemporaries. It depends in large part on how often people invoke his name or his accomplishments after his tenure is completed. Giants in industry are still referred to decades after their departure, such as Thomas Edison, Andrew Carnegie, George Eastman, and Alfred Sloan. In many companies, even though the leader was largely unknown to society, that person is still spoken of and regarded highly many years after his or her retirement. This measure can only be left to posterity.

The disadvantage of measures that are based on long-term results only, or lagging measures, such as those described above, is that they give little guidance to anyone seeking to grow leadership skills in the here and now. By the time these judgments are made, the individual has usually moved on to other pursuits. From a practical point of view, a leader needs more immediate measures of impact if these measures are to serve any purpose. Finding real-time measures would be more meaningful since they would permit the individual to profit from them.

Measurement in leadership serves its greatest function when it is used to establish causal relationships between leader behavior and follower behavior. Measurement should help a leader answer the questions, "What must I do to cause this number to change?" "What is the effect on the number when I do this?" This assumes that you can count something since a judgment would not offer you the same benefit. When you are rating or ranking some event or impact, the nature of the question changes. "What must I do to cause that opinion to change?" or "What is the effect on their opinion when I do this?" While these may be important considerations, since they are judgments, they are indirect measures of an event or activity and as such are subject to interpretation. Whenever possible, actual counts are preferred to judgments.

When we measure leadership, then, we want to use numbers wherever possible. These numbers must pertain to follower behavior. Our question then becomes, "How do I get more people to do X?" These sorts of numbers will provide a baseline on your exercise of leadership in the past, as well as a tool for determining the effect your personal actions create in others.

The best predictors of leadership are found in the behavior of the leader's followers. The most powerful predictors fall into four categories:

1. How do the followers respond to the leader's direction?
2. How focused are the followers on the leader's goals?
3. How do the followers relate to each other?
4. How do the followers react to the leader?

The first of these measures is concerned with how effectively the leader brings about change: once the leader puts out a new idea or proposal, how quickly does it gain momentum? This behavioral momentum is a function of the mass, velocity, and direction of follower efforts. This category applies to everyone and in any situation. It is at the very core of leadership. Do you have followers? Are people working to please you or merely to avoid your displeasure? Are they responding to your leadership or to your authority? Are they doing what they are doing because they want to or because they must? We repeat that we are aware that sometimes authority must be exercised, but the exception should not become the rule. Which more frequently occurs in your workplace—leadership or coercion?

The second category concerns itself with the execution of core practices: how well do the followers perform their tasks, whether those tasks are routine or new? While it may happen that the leader requires the followers to jettison all of their past practices, this is extremely rare. When the execution of any change initiative interferes with the ability of the organization to produce its product or services, success becomes problematic.

The third category describes the cultural impact of the leader's practices: How well do the followers relate to the cause and to each other? Has the leader created a workplace where followers are willing to sacrifice personal short-term goals in order to help a peer or another work unit accomplish theirs? Effective leaders tend to the relationships between followers so that precious energy is not sapped by internal conflict and ineffective processes.

The fourth area of measurement comes from the way the followers behave toward the leader: Are they comfortable enough with the leader that they will seek guidance for not only business matters but personal ones as well? Are they comfortable enough with the leader that they will admit to mistakes before the leader finds out about them? Is the leader a mentor? How many leaders does the leader create?

Collectively, these indicators provide the best possible forecast of the leader's impact on the growth of the business, on the customers and the marketplace, and on his or her legacy. To gather measures that will give leaders the best opportunity to make changes in their behavior, each of these four categories should generate three counts of behavior for a total of 12 counts. While all measures, by definition, are historical snapshots, these 12 get us close enough to the action to provide ample opportunity to learn from them and to alter the future. We must truly focus on these measures if we are to take the real measure of a leader.

chapter 9

MEASURING FOLLOWER RESPONSE
IN-PROCESS MEASURES OF LEADERSHIP

The best mirror is an old friend.

George Herbert
Jacula Prudentum (1651)

Our leadership measures are comprised of four categories with three measures each.

I. *Momentum*	III. *Initiative*
1. Mass	7. Teamwork
2. Velocity	8. Interfaces
3. Direction	9. Innovation
II. *Commitment*	IV. *Reciprocity*
4. Vision	10. Trust
5. Values	11. Respect
6. Persistence	12. Growth

Momentum

The laws of the universe have their correlates in human behavior (Nevin, 1988). While these laws require some modification when applying them to people, the underlying principles are very instructive. Physics has many ways of describing change, which interests us because change is how we measure leadership. In physics, some force must act on some mass to produce a change in velocity of that mass or a change in its direction. When speaking of followers, either collectively or singly, we can see that these same concepts apply. In any undertaking where we wish to create change, we must either get people to change their behavior from past practices to new ones, get them to change the pace of their current behavior, or we must change the number of people who are committing energy and effort to the objective. The force that creates this change in momentum is leadership.

In physics, if we know something about a change in the velocity and direction of a mass, we have a great deal of information about the force that produced it. In chemistry, if we know something about a change in the mass of something, we will probably know something about the forces that brought it about, which keeps that mass coherent. Leadership is that force which binds followers together to form a critical mass, which changes the velocity of that mass, and which moves that mass in a different direction. The first measures of leadership, then, are related to the momentum of the followers. They are mass, velocity, and direction.

1. MASS

HOW MANY FOLLOWERS RESPOND TO THE LEADER'S CALL?

Before you can quantify this aspect of follower behavior, you must first distinguish between compliance behavior and discretionary behavior. Even slaves get up and move when the slave driver gives the command! The issue in leadership is the extra effort that the followers give. If the followers limit their response just to meeting the leader's requirements, the term *leader* is misapplied. Intrinsic to leadership is voluntary effort.

It is the true discriminator between leadership and compulsion or obligation.

Typically, discretionary effort is not captured in organizations. In part that is because it is expected. Yet our experience is that, in the absence of leadership, discretionary effort does not occur as frequently as is required. Organizations that survive in the absence of individual initiative are called bureaucracies and are characterized by low levels of follower energy and enthusiasm. Bureaucracies can be transformed, as can any organization, when leadership brings out the best in the followers.

Discretionary effort does not mean heroic or extraordinary effort. The opportunities for that kind of behavior arise only infrequently. Discretionary effort means that individuals simply do more than they are required by the job description or by their management. Discretionary effort can, and should, be found in anyone, anywhere in the organization. Very few, if any, performance appraisal systems ask for the number of followers who give more than is required; yet it is an important indicator of leadership.

The question for leaders is, *"If I were to go down a list of my followers, what percentage is delivering discretionary effort?"*

2. Velocity

How long does it take for the followers to take action?

Our experience in business and industry has convinced us that the most common management methodology is management by nagging. Policy, procedures, and regulations proliferate exactly because they do not produce the desired response. The usual reaction to this slow or indifferent response is to repeat what has been said longer, louder, and meaner. On the other hand, when effective leadership is present, relatively little effort is required to get followers to respond. We know that speed of execution is a competitive advantage in almost any market. Internally, then, this speed of response by the followers is a hallmark of effective leadership.

Julius Caesar is probably one of the more outstanding exemplars of this aspect of leadership. His attention to the daily aspects of his soldiers' lives and training produced in them abilities which were superior to those of their foes, and even of other Roman soldiers serving under different commanders. Some of the most extraordinary feats of Caesar's enemies were merely commonplace to Caesar's Legions. His entire army could march and maneuver with such speed that enemy commanders could not lend credence to the reports of their spies when they reported on Caesar's movements.

Once a decision is made by the leader, and the follower understands the expectations, we look at how much time elapses before they act on that decision. In larger organizations, this is measured in layers: first the leader's direct reports, then the levels of management, the layers of supervision, and finally at the front line where the critical behaviors occur. We first measure from top to bottom of the organization and then use the measures of the intervening layers to troubleshoot communications speed and accuracy.

Since leadership is all about followers' discretionary effort, we are looking for evidence that the followers are making an effort to understand the directive and to accurately respond to it. Our measure of speed focuses on time to action. This measure can be applied to any initiative that the leader selects but the more critical the initiative, the more important rapid execution becomes.

The question for leaders is, *"If I were to announce a requirement for action, how quickly would I get discretionary effort at all levels of the organization?"*

3. DIRECTION

HOW CLOSELY DO THE BEHAVIORS OF THE FOLLOWERS MATCH THE LEADER'S PRIORITIES?

This measure is closely intertwined with velocity. It is not enough that the followers engage in high levels of activity, as rate of activity can often be misleading. In his book *Human Competence* (1996), Thomas Gilbert offers his Leisurely Theorems of Management which state that exemplars are rarely the most active of your followers. Through extended practice and high levels of competence, exemplars find ways to outperform others while actually exerting less effort. We know this to be true of many athletes, where the outstanding performers make truly difficult tasks appear to be effortless.

The true measure here is how quickly followers engage in the behaviors that move the initiative forward. In some cases this requires the individual to try the behaviors the leader has identified before they can figure out which behaviors are truly critical. Velocity demonstrates the follower's willingness to be led, whereas direction demonstrates the clarity of communications.

There are many reasons that followers might engage in either high levels of behavior in pursuit of non-contributing activities or why they might not become actively engaged in the leaders' plans. Measuring activity against the leaders priorities will help you identify punishers, obstacles, and distractions, all of which work against leadership effectiveness.

This measurement should be taken multiple times throughout the duration of any initiative. You will soon discern a pattern that shows how long it typically takes for the followers to create momentum for the leader's plans.

The question for leaders is, *"What percentage of people focuses effort on the top priority actions that drive my requirements?"*

Commitment

Leadership is much more than just creating momentum. Many people with contagious enthusiasm can begin something that peters out as the initial level of excitement dies down. Leadership requires that the momentum be maintained until the objective is reached, which is often only when new practices have become a part of the daily routine.

Commitment is related, but not identical, to momentum. Once movement has begun and the followers have taken action, the laws of physics describe the conditions which will cancel out that progress.

Friction, the energy loss that will stop motion, has its counterpart in human effort as well. It comes from many sources and is commonly referred to as *resistance to change*. Leadership is required to offset this loss of energy and to maintain the effort. The result of the leader's effort is commitment, the intensity and the focus of the followers' actions over time. And any leader can see this intensity and focus, or lack thereof, by interacting with the followers.

Jürgen Schrempp the Chairman of the Board of Daimler-Chrysler, the seventh largest corporation in the world, recently pointed out that "even the Chairman of the Board needs to be at the scene of the action" (Taylor, 2005). There is no other way to know what the real capabilities of the organization are and to know how well people are executing the plan.

But, just as MBWA (Management by Walking Around), the idea articulated by Thomas Peters and Robert Waterman (1982) in *In Search of Excellence*, was misapplied by so many, leaders can do damage by their interactions with followers who do not report directly to them. It is important for the leader to remember that his purpose is to analyze his leadership structure and effectiveness, not micromanage follower activity. And, this analysis should focus on the most important attributes of that structure—the persistence of the followers in following the vision and applying the organization's values to their daily work.

Consciously competent leaders are always searching for specific kinds of intelligence that gives them direction as to what they, the leaders, must do next. At the scene of the action, leaders are seeking to know the level of commitment of the followers to the vision and values the leader has espoused and their persistence in pursuit of the leader's objectives. Our measures of commitment are vision, values, and persistence.

4. Vision

HOW MANY PEOPLE CAN RELATE THEIR EFFORTS TO THE LEADER'S VISION?

This is all about focus and the ability of the followers to maintain that focus over time. Are the followers doing those things that will maintain momentum for the plan and lead to its success? As the newness of the plan and the initial enthusiasm it produces wears off, do the individuals involved keep their focus or does their commitment to its success evaporate? At some point, all followers must make choices about their behavior in the absence of specific directions. The purpose of the vision is to provide guidance on how to make those choices.

If you were to go to the scene of the action and ask, "Why are you doing that?" you expect an answer that relates back to the big picture or the vision. It is not enough that the leader makes the connection. The vision only acts as a guide when the individual can connect her actions to the vision. Jack Gordon, a client from Rubbermaid, once visited another client, Preston Trucking, to observe how they managed their people. His visit took him to a loading dock where a forklift driver happened to be moving Rubbermaid product. As the forklift passed, Jack said to the driver, "Careful son! I work for Rubbermaid." Without a pause, the driver replied, "So do I, sir!" Do your followers understand the implications of their daily tasks as well? There are two components to this measure: can the followers articulate the vision *and* do their actions demonstrate their understanding? We have observed many times that words and actions often do not coincide.

The question for leaders is, *"What percentage of the followers can relate their efforts to the vision?"*

5. VALUES

HOW MANY PEOPLE CAN RELATE AN EXAMPLE EXEMPLIFYING THE LEADER'S VALUES?

Overzealous followers can destroy the legacy of a leader. An unethical, immoral, or illegal act by a follower can put the leader in the position of having to prove that she did not promote or condone such acts. Since followers so often imitate the behavior of their leader, there is often the presumption that, at a minimum, the follower is simply copying what he has observed the leader do. This is one of the reasons leaders should promote ethical behavior at every opportunity.

Values are most often observed in the breach rather than in the many everyday actions that go unnoticed. Unless the follower reports situations of conflict between the needs of the individual or the needs of the business and the values of the leader, it is unlikely that anyone will be aware of the choice that person made. Also, unless the individual reports on his ethical conflict, no one will learn from his experience except for him, if he learns from it at all.

Simply talking about values is not necessarily useful. Talk is not a reliable predictor of behavior. Talk is valuable for clarifying examples and non-examples of ethical conduct but for most people the conversation does not lead to behavior change. On the other hand, when an individual can relate an example of a person acting in an ethical manner, they are more likely to be influenced to act in a similar way. If they accurately relate their own dilemma and their subsequent choice, the resulting recognition by others is more likely to help them make similar, tougher choices in the future.

Each part of this hierarchy is valuable. Talk about ethics sensitizes people to the issues and makes them more likely to recognize ethical choices. Hearing others relate their ethical situations helps the listener identify similar situations and makes it more likely that they will model their choice on that of the example. Relating your own situation, when it leads to recognition, makes it more likely that you will act ethically in the future. So the more examples the followers can cite, the more likely the other individuals within the organization are to act ethically. And, when exceptions are found, the more likely the people within the organization are to recognize it as an exception and not part of some pattern condoned by the leader.

This is a more complex measure than some of the others because there are so many qualifiers. Most organization's value statements contain several values, not just one. Values relate to your decisions as well as to your actions, so these measures must be taken to correlate your values to your policies, procedures, strategies, and tactics.

The question for leaders is, *"What percentage of followers can cite an organization's decision or a current example of conduct exemplifying the organization's values?"*

6. PERSISTENCE

HOW MANY PEOPLE MEET THEIR COMMITMENTS?

We usually think of persistence as a characteristic of the leader. The persistence of the follower is an equally important factor. We worked in a plant where the plant manager asked for volunteers to lead a new initiative. One person immediately stood up and agreed to take it on. Later, when nothing had been done, our consultant asked the volunteer why he had accepted the task. He replied that management never followed up on things, so volunteering was safe. They would remember his readiness to help, but apparently not his lack of follow through. This is actually a fairly common approach to leadership's initiatives. Most places where we work have a *program du jour,* or flavor of the month approach to change. The skepticism this creates adds to the effort required and leads many people to believe in the myth that people resist change. With good leadership, followers continue the new practices until given a new direction. Effective productive habits are then the norm rather than the exception.

The Matching Law, discovered by Dr. Richard Herrnstein (1997), shows that people will allocate their behavior to activities in exact proportion to the value derived from each. In other words, behavior goes to the most reinforcing part of the environment at any moment in time. It is the most powerful formula in all of behavior analysis, and shows that when everything is important, nothing is important. For people to know which behaviors to persist in, leaders must intentionally limit the focus of their effort. They create core expectations that define excellence and use these as the primary indicators of follower response.

It is tempting to measure follower persistence simply as a measure of follower success, and that is certainly a significant part of it. But persistence covers failure as well. Our company worked with a research and development organization that celebrated its failures. They considered it a success when an idea had been pursued to the point where it was clear that it could not become a profitable product. By acknowledging a dead end as soon as possible, time, money, and resources were freed up and could be redirected into other, and more profitable, pursuits.

But this kind of failure is a failure of the plan, not a failure of execution. *Persistence* is a term that implies continual, forceful action in the direction of the goal; an effort that is not blocked by minor obstacles. With this in mind, a reasonable approximation of persistence is a measure of the number of individuals and units that meet or beat milestones and objectives.

The standard by which to measure persistence is the leader's behavior. While anyone would hope that the followers would exceed the leader's level of enthusiasm, this is not the norm. One of the earliest indicators of failure is when the leader must expend greater levels of energy than the followers on an initiative. On the other hand, leaders know that they must demonstrate high levels of interest and enthusiasm, over time, for significant undertakings. Jack Welch demonstrated the highest levels of involvement in Six Sigma for years, even promoting it after his retirement. As a result, GE's leadership has embedded that practice into its culture and Six Sigma continues to be a vital management methodology to this day.

An important interim measure of persistence is found by answering the question, "How many things that we start do we finish?" Where initiatives tend to wither away, people learn to abandon commitments. Tracking commitments that you and your staff make to each other and quantifying the percentage that is met will tell you a great deal about your organization and your followers' persistence.

The question for the leader is, *"At intervals, such as milestones and deadlines, what percentage of performers demonstrates continuous energy and enthusiasm for the leader's initiatives?"*

Initiative

Even when individuals can do better work alone than with a team, we expect them to seek out opportunities to help others and gain advantages from the synergies made possible through cooperative efforts.

This is a form of initiative that requires direct intervention and promotion by the leader since the most valuable consequences in organizations come from personal effort. The rewards available for individual effort are diluted when multiple performers are involved. Any situation that encourages competition, for example, works against cooperation.

Sacrifice—when we choose to defer our own preferences so that another person can have theirs—is implicit in all good relationships. If sacrifice is either absent or is only made by one party, friction builds up which ultimately interferes with the ability to work together. The more time spent adjudicating disputes, the less likely it is that leadership is present.

Leaders foster peer relationships to create an environment that encourages individuals and groups to make contributions rather than simply follow orders. When peers work well together, they encourage and support each other. When these same peers buy into the leader's vision, they also challenge and correct each other. These conditions support initiative and innovation and make the organization more adaptable to changing conditions, which makes it more successful.

John Hunt, professor of organizational behavior at London Business School, makes the point that the "top team is a better predictor of company performance than the chief executive." He contends that "in the most successful companies, the leadership role is not a person but a core of four or five people. Their day-to-day work is highly individual. They trust each other implicitly. Allocation of tasks is based on individual strengths, not weaknesses. The core members continually give each other feedback" (2001). This group, the leader's staff, and its work are the first challenge of leadership. And, it is a powerful predictor of the other measures.

The measures of initiative are teamwork, interfaces, and innovation.

7. TEAMWORK

HOW FREQUENTLY DO INDIVIDUALS ASSIST THEIR PEERS?

This may be a difficult number to get at but it highlights the issue.

Cooperation, as with any other behavior, must be reinforced if it is to continue. If we don't recognize it when it happens, we leave its continuation to chance. If we can't tell whether it is happening more or less frequently, we should assume that it is not happening often enough. Changing voluntary cooperation from a random event to habitual practice is another leadership challenge.

The benefits to the leader of promoting teamwork are many. The most important is that teamwork creates a more reinforcing environment, where individuals seek each other out for input in their decision making. This creates a work setting where a significant amount of self-correcting activity occurs, minimizing the frequency of errors, and the need for management intervention.

A lack of cooperation is evidence that the leader's goals are less important than those of the followers. Possible causes are either that the vision is not compelling or the leader is inadvertently promoting actions that reduce initiative. While other explanations are possible, these are significant enough that the leader must get to the root of this issue. As with any root-cause analysis, numbers allow you to ask the right questions.

The question for leaders is, *"How many acts of cooperation or assistance from peers can my followers relate?"*

8. INTERFACES

HOW MANY UNITS ACTIVELY ASSIST OTHER UNITS?

It is common for processes to be suboptimized by optimizing the individual parts. We have often seen one manager increase his department's productivity only to see the plant output drop as his increase creates or exposes bottlenecks in other departments. This situation creates either heroes, martyrs, or scapegoats. All of these situations lead to finger-pointing, which increases internal tension and conflict. This, in turn, saps the leader's time and energy.

It is a leadership function to ensure that all units of the organization interface with each other effectively. The higher up the organization, the more critical this is. Unit boundaries form the walls of silos only too easily and present obstacles for the most effective utilization of resources. When units proactively seek opportunities to assist other units, boundaries are minimized as ways are found to optimize achievement of organizational objectives.

This is another measure that is rarely captured in organizations. Once again, the assumption is that units will cooperate for the common good. However, we remind you that these assumptions, when untested, form a poor basis for leadership beliefs and practices.

The question for leaders is, *"How many followers can relate acts of cooperation and assistance from other internal units?"*

9. INNOVATION

HOW MANY SUGGESTIONS ARE MADE
THAT SUPPORT THE MISSION OR THE VISION?

Just as discretionary effort is the lifeblood of leadership, innovation is its most visible manifestation. Suggestions for improvement are one way most people can contribute and express their support for the leader's goals. When leaders support or promote programs such as Six Sigma or the Toyota Way, they are harnessing the power of follower suggestions and channeling it into useful purposes. Organizations where the concept of leadership is summarized by the power and control of the leader usually fail in these efforts.

The willingness to offer opinion and advice on better ways to pursue the vision is extremely fragile. All it takes is for someone in authority to ignore, critique, or reject suggestions for most people to decide to keep their ideas to themselves. They do not, however, forget the idea, but instead, judge management for its failure to pursue a course of action which, to the person suggesting it, seems so sensible. This weakens their attachment to the leader and his cause over time.

Granted, not all suggestions have value to the organization. But this form of contributing to the cause still must be encouraged. The more competitive the industry, the more critical it is to distinguish the organization and its products through innovation. And, since competitors can so easily and so quickly copy these innovations, remaining a leader depends on more contributions from more followers. Where suggestions are concerned, the quantity of ideas is a predictor of the number of useful ideas.

The question for leaders is, *"What percentage of followers offers multiple suggestions in support of the mission and vision?"*

Reciprocity

Nothing so bedevils would-be leaders as the nature of their relationship with their followers. There are so many wrong-headed beliefs about this relationship that many individuals cripple themselves from the outset. One example is the executive who stated that he "was not paid to be well-liked." While it is true that leadership is not about popularity; anyone expecting discretionary effort from people who do not like and trust him is engaging in a Sisyphean effort. (Sisyphus was an ancient Greek king condemned by the gods for his insolence to roll a rock to the top of a mountain. As he neared the top, the rock would fall back to the bottom and Sisyphus would have to begin again. This cycle was to be repeated for eternity.)

The same is true of leaders who do not believe it is their job to train their followers. They treat their direct reports like replaceable cogs in a machine when they make statements such as, "If I have to tell him what to do, I don't need him!" Expecting followers to read your mind is a self-defeating game, yet many people play it. No leader can be more successful than the combined successes of his followers.

Leaders who fail to establish the right relationship with their followers condemn themselves to perpetual work. They become more and more like a prison guard, always suspicious that they are not getting full measure for their benevolence, and continually trying to find the flaw or fault in their subordinates' work before it is exposed to the world. This need to know everything and to check everyone's work is self-defeating in the long run and destroys one's legacy. No one wants to tell positive stories about their prison guard. They only delight in telling stories that highlight the guard's shortcomings and that show the guard in a negative light. The measures of effective leader/follower interactions are trust, respect, and growth.

10. TRUST

HOW OFTEN DO FOLLOWERS TAKE RESPONSIBILITY FOR MISTAKES?

No one can command trust; it must be earned. In addition, trust can never be taken for granted. All leaders must earn the trust of their followers and work to keep it. Without trust, more energy will go into preparing defenses than will go into the strategic and tactical aspects of the business. Whenever people are concerned about the hidden agenda of the leader, politics will come to dominate their activities.

The single most telling indication of trust is to see to whom someone will confess a fault or failure. If they know how the other person will use the information they reveal and that it will not be used against them, most people are quite willing to tell even embarrassing details about themselves. When they distrust the other person to use the knowledge wisely, they withhold all but the minimum information necessary. This is damaging both to the organization and to the individual. Gaps in our knowledge of the causes of successes and failures inhibit learning and in some situations, because of those gaps, we learn things that aren't true.

Many leaders know how to get individuals to relate their failures and mistakes so they can learn from them. Peter Senge (1990) wrote about the Learning Organization, where a basic feature was how to profit from mistakes. Hiding and denying are dangerous tendencies that leaders must root out and replace with telling and revealing so that the mechanisms of success and failure are shared with all.

The question for leaders is, *"What percentage of the followers shares failures or mistakes with peers and the leader?"*

11. RESPECT

HOW OFTEN DO FOLLOWERS SEEK OUT
THE LEADER FOR ADVICE OR COUNSEL?

The people we identify as our leaders are people we expect to lead us to greater success than we would achieve on our own. We attribute some advantage to them over our own abilities whether it is in judgment, knowledge, contacts, resources, or some other useful attribute. By selecting a person as a leader, followers choose to defer to that person in those areas. It is only natural then that, when confronted with choices and decisions, we would approach her for input and guidance.

By the same token, if we fear someone, we try to avoid being in that person's presence. If we are forced to be in their presence, we limit our contributions to those that are necessary, while trying to keep our exposure to a minimum. We will create reasons for this minimum contact and may even find ways to keep the leader from approaching us. This is the genesis of the accusation of micromanaging. We do not welcome the contact as we perceive the person to be a punisher.

In contrast, when a leader is supportive and encouraging, individuals share more of their work and more of their lives than would otherwise ever be known. With this more intimate level of knowledge of the follower, the leader has an even greater ability to direct the follower's efforts and to inspire ever greater achievements.

Obviously, caution must be taken with this measure. Some individuals will seek advice to evade their own responsibility in case of failure and some people will seek out the leader to curry favor. For these and other reasons, judgment plays a bigger role in this measure than we like. However, with more contact, the leader who is self-aware will quickly learn the motivation of the person seeking advice and will determine whether it is based on that person's respect for the leader or for some other reason.

The question for the leader is, *"How many followers initiate contact with the leader seeking counsel or input to personal and professional decisions?"*

12. GROWTH

HOW MANY FOLLOWERS BECOME LEADERS?

If you want to maximize your impact, lead leaders! Leadership is always about the personal influence one person exercises with another. Leaders are always limited by their ability to communicate with, and personally relate to, their followers. If each of your followers, in turn, leads others, your impact is multiplied.

Effective leaders recognize that every interaction is an opportunity to develop their followers. They do not perform their subordinates' work for them, such as directing, correcting, or rewarding the subordinates' reports, except in urgent circumstances. They do not micromanage. The task is to teach the subordinates how to perform their work most effectively. Doing it for them robs followers of an opportunity to practice and to learn. The outcome of effective leadership is that subordinates increase their ability and willingness to lead others in the desired direction.

Not only does effective leadership produce more leaders, it also produces more individuals who strive to improve their ability to contribute to the leader's vision. In many cases, this is demonstrated simply by the number of people who volunteer and competently perform work outside of their current job responsibility. It is also seen in the number of individuals who are given more significant opportunities to utilize the skills and knowledge acquired as a result of contact with the leader, whether inside or outside of the organization. The best leaders produce the most new leaders. Though delayed and inadequate, another measure of leadership is the number of subordinates given greater responsibility within the organization and the number who are selected for opportunities to lead in other organizations. Good leaders do not hold people back.

The question for leaders is, *"How many managers of your unit have you actively promoted inside and outside of the organization?"*

LEADERSHIP MEASUREMENT OPTIONS

. . . we have to remember that what we observe
is not nature in itself but nature exposed to our method of questioning.

Werner Karl Heisenberg (1958)

Since we have defined leadership as the followers' response to the leader, leader and follower behaviors then are linked and are interdependent variables. What the leader does determines the follower's response and the follower's response defines the leader's next, necessary behaviors. In measuring leadership Heisenberg's Uncertainty Principle (1927) is relevant. That is, the more precisely we measure one variable, the more uncertainty we have about the other. Thus, the more precisely we measure the follower response, the less certain we are about which of the leader's behaviors actually produced it.

For our purposes, this suggests that precision in measurement, while important, is not critical. We must compromise on the accuracy of our measures so that the focus remains on the relationship of the two variables and we do not become too absorbed by either variable alone. Historically, the measures of follower response have been taken only at the most general level. This does not allow the observer to determine how changes in one variable produce changes in the other.

Our suggestions on ways to measure leadership, then, are simply a first approximation. With this, we shed light on the leadership functioning in such a way that we may progress toward other, more cogent measures. Developing the perfect set of measures is always a process of refining what we already have. If you wait until you have the perfect measures, you will simply wait. And as you wait, significant opportunities for learning and growth are lost.

Ways to Measure Leadership

In measuring things, you either count them or you judge them. Counting is the preferred method and is the way we measure when the performance is critical. The less important the issue, the less inclined we are to count. Judgment is the methodology we use when we are not willing to expend the resources to find the count. This does not mean that judgment does not have value, only that it is a less accurate approach to quantification.

When we judge leadership, we give our opinion of it. While this is obviously important, it has limited value as feedback. The reason is that opinion always has two components: the behavior observed and the value placed on the observed behavior. In response to the feedback, does the person being judged focus on changing the behavior or on changing the opinion? Unfortunately, we find too often that changing only one behavior does not change the opinion in a class of behaviors being judged as opposed to the critical behavior needed to produce a different outcome. We might, for instance, start coming to meetings on time in response to feedback that we were unprofessional only to find that being late was only one of many behaviors of concern to our evaluator. We have thus changed one behavior, but not the other person's opinion.

Judgments are always enhanced as feedback when based on concrete criteria. Thus, feedback that says someone is not decisive is less helpful than feedback that identifies the issue as having action items that are overdue awaiting your decision. Saying that someone is a poor communicator is less helpful than telling him that his written communications do not state specific expectations of the reader. Judging people as arrogant is not as helpful as telling them that they do not acknowledge people who have opinions that differ from their own.

The more concrete the criteria, the more helpful your opinion is to others. Their response to the feedback is, in turn, more immediate and more focused. The more often the criteria are used, the better the feedback giver can refine the criteria so that feedback is truly helpful. Used frequently enough, this leads to counting behaviors, which is the most effective way to help people change (Daniels and Daniels, 2004).

We always recommend counts even when you can only sample the behavior. Our chief concern with sampling is the trigger for the count. If you count exceptions to desired performance, the most common way of sampling behavior, you typically have little useful information that will put these events in perspective.

Measurement Formats

There are numerous ways to gain feedback on leadership. Our four choices (of the many options) are surveys, checklists, behavior counts, and matrices.

SURVEYS

Since the measure of a leader is the followers, we can always ask the followers for feedback. A survey is the most common way to do this. The basic format is to ask their opinion about the specific dimensions of interest. It takes skill, however, to phrase the questions to avoid prejudicing the answers. We have the same issues of reliability when we ask about opinion, so the criteria must be specific to elicit focused responses.

Questions can be phrased in many ways. We have selected two ways: as the individual's personal response to the leader or as the individual's perception of the response of the other performers. We find that both are useful in creating a richer view of the followers' response to the leader.

Yes/No (counts) responses:

1. When you know that X is responsible, do you put any extra efforts into his/her initiatives?

2. When X asks you to do something, do you start on it right away?

3. Are you working now on his/her top priority issues?

4. Do you see the connection between your daily efforts and the organization's vision?

5. Can you cite an example of someone living the organization's values?

6. Do you invest as much energy and enthusiasm as the leader invests into his/her initiatives?

7. Can you give a recent example where a peer has helped you with your work?

8. Do other departments and work units cooperate and assist your unit?

9. How many suggestions for improvement have you made within the last three months?

10. Is it safe to admit that you have made a mistake or failed at something?

11. Is X someone you feel you would respect for counsel and advice?

12. Are you actively encouraged to improve your skills and personal growth here?

Using the same survey format, you can ask individuals their perception of their peers. This is helpful because some people tend to edit their responses to questions about their personal behavior, but might be more open to telling their perception of the group's response to the leader. Some sample questions:

1. Do your peers think of X as a leader?
2. When X asks your work unit to do something, do they usually start work on it right away?
3. Do your peers assist each other in their work?
4. Does the leader encourage individuals to improve their knowledge and abilities?

If these questions are changed slightly, you can get a score, or a rating. The most common scale is 1-10 but a scale of 0-10 or 1-6 is more useful as there is no midpoint and the rater must choose one end of the scale over the other. However, a scale of 1-10 is usually chosen since calculations (percentage) are easier and more aligned with those of our educational system.

RATE RESPONSES										
10 = Best Score										
	1	2	3	4	5	6	7	8	9	10
1. How effective do you consider X as a leader?										
2. How willing are you to follow X when he asks you to do something you have not done before?										
3. How quickly do you respond to, and do, what X tells you to do?										
4. How well do people act and make decisions based on the values of the organization?										

These are some issues you should consider if you choose to do a survey.

1. Have you worded the questions so that no bias is suggested toward a particular answer?
2. Is the survey administered by someone the respondents trust?
3. Is anonymity assured for the responder?
4. Do enough people respond that the feedback is representative of all followers?
5. Are you committed to doing something with the feedback?
6. How will the respondents know that you got their message?

SAMPLING

One of the simplest and easiest ways to measure leadership is to record yes and no as you observe your own behavior or follower behavior. This involves determining which indicators are of interest and then actively looking for them. If, for example, you want to measure interactions with your direct reports, you might list the indicators of respect, trust, and growth and do an inventory. Have any of your direct reports discussed some failure or shortcoming with you within the last month? Which ones? Have any of them talked to you about their personal interests during that interval? Who? Have you actively discussed the positive accomplishments of any of your followers to people in significant organizational positions? Which ones?

This inventory will reveal much about this facet of your relationship with your followers. By the same token, it should prompt you to take actions that encourage these behaviors on your followers' part. Checklists, much as To Do lists, encourage the observer to be more proactive in discovering opportunities for change and in taking steps to capitalize on those opportunities.

BEHAVIOR COUNTS

Counting the frequency of behavior is a very useful tool if used correctly. It provides more frequent feedback which will accelerate your learning. Here, too, we recommend two types of counting:

1. Track your own impact on your followers.

2. Followers record their own interactions with their peers and subordinates.

If you track your own behavior and remember that it is the response of the followers that counts, you might learn about the level of commitment by asking these questions.

COMMITMENT LEVEL	
MY BEHAVIOR	FOLLOWER BEHAVIOR
1. How many people did I ask today to tell me the vision? How many could state it?	1. Could I state the vision?
2. How many people did I ask today to give me an example of someone following our values? How many could name someone and tell what they had done?	2. Could I give an example of someone following the company values? Could I name and tell what they had done?
3. How many people did I ask today about a commitment that was due? How many had met it?	3. Did I talk about a commitment that was due? Did I meet the commitment?

If you asked your direct reports to track their own behaviors, you might learn a great deal about peer relationships. Remember to encourage and reinforce honest answers.

1. How many of your peers volunteered their help this week?

2. How many examples can you cite of other units assisting your department this week?

3. How many people in your unit suggested something that promoted the vision or the accomplishment of your mission?

Of course you could also ask them to rate how well these things are being done, but this tends to be an infrequent measure and would not create the same contingencies for supporting these behaviors within your organization. As with all measures, the more often we are forced to acknowledge some behavior, the more sensitive we are to that same behavior and the more likely we are to notice it when it does occur. Ratings do not force that same level of attention to detail and rely more on impressions than on facts.

MATRIX

Another tool which we find helpful is the matrix. Many organizations use it as a scorecard, but these are usually focused on measures of results, not on follower behavior. To get ongoing measures of follower behavior, you must invest time and resources; the payoff will more than justify any costs.

One of the primary values of a matrix is that it gives you a single number, or score, so that you can see progress even when multiple variables are being tracked. As complex as leadership is, it's possible to improve on one or two behaviors during one interval, but regress on another during the same time. The matrix will give context to your efforts so that you can get an overall picture of your success and your improvement.

The key elements of a matrix are the variables being measured, the weighting assigned to each variable, the standards or goals you are being measured against, and a method for translating performance on each behavior against that standard or goal into a weighted performance score. These will permit you to see trends in your personal impact on the organization (Daniels and Daniels, 2004).

The example on the following page shows how you might set up a matrix on your leadership where the results are attained through a survey (Daniels and Daniels 2004).

We recommend that you set your standards or goals based on your first survey. There are no real standards as there are few organizations or leaders who measure follower behavior. Therefore, we suggest that you establish a baseline with your first survey and use that as part of your goal-setting process. It's important to know that 13 on the scale is rarely achieved. It is analogous to the world record. A 13 is not a guess, but represents a true benchmark set by the best example of leadership available to you. Your goal is to move in that direction. The trend is more important than the actual score. If you are improving your score, you're having a greater impact on the organization through your followers' behavior.

SAMPLE PERFORMANCE MATRIX

Name _____ Position _____ Manager _____ Date _____

BEHAVIOR PINPOINTS	4	5	6	7	8	9	10	11	12	13	X Weight	Points
Followers delivering discretionary effort	25%	27%		33%	37%	44%	50%	60%	67%	75%	90	
How long it takes to start work on my initiative		3 days		2 days		1 day	same day	4 hrs.		1 hr.	80	
Followers focusing on my top priorities	11%	15%	21%	33%	40%	50%	60%	70%	75%	85%	90	
Followers acting to promote the vision	25%		33%		40%		50%	60%	67%	75%	90	
Followers who can cite an example of the values	25%		33%				50%	60%	67%	75%	90	
Followers who demonstrate energy for progress on key initiatives	25%		33%				50%	60%	67%	75%	80	
Followers who say we help each other	10%	50%	55%	60%	65%	70%	75%	80%	85%	95%	80	
Followers who say other units assist them	20%		33%				50%	60%	67%	75%	80	
Followers who offer more than one suggestion	5%	10%	20%	33%	45%	50%	60%	60%	80%	90%	80	
Followers who show they can openly state their opinions	15%	20%	25%	33%	40%	45%	50%	60%	67%	75%	90	
Followers who share their failures or mistakes with peers and the leader	5%	10%	15%	20%	25%	30%	35%	40%	45%	55%	80	
Followers who state they are encouraged to grow	25%		33%				60%	75%	80%	95%	80	
SCORE												

chapter 11

MOTIVATING FOLLOWERS

The applause of a single human being is of great consequence.

Samuel Johnson (1780)

Leaders have the responsibility for creating a work environment that causes people to do their best every day. In theory this should be simple, since the overwhelming majority of employees are willing workers. Only an extremely small number of people take a job expecting to get paid for minimal effort. Most people, by the act of taking a job, demonstrate that they want to do it well. We find that many companies squander this goodwill through their leadership practices. Apparently, it is easier to lose discretionary effort than it is to build it.

If people are willing to perform at their best and they don't, where does the problem lie? Dr. Edwards Deming, the noted quality guru, attributed well over 90% of the problems of quality not to front-line employees, but to management. We certainly agree and we extend this to most other performance deficiencies as well. The same leadership practices that throw away the employee's goodwill also create the climate that suboptimizes organizational effectiveness.

Leaders create the culture, the place, and the conditions for employees and their work. This includes the physical conditions and the management process. The most effective leaders first look at those elements before looking to individuals or groups of employees for assigning blame or attempting a fix. Most failures of organizations are failures of the management process, not employees' behavior. Although most organizations have some form of process management, few can specify their behavior management process. Indeed, supervisors and managers are often advised to find a management style that fits their personality and the situation. Because there are so many different personality types and possible situations in an organization, there will be many different solutions to the same problem. No effective, stable leadership process is possible with this number of uncontrolled management variables.

An effective management process causes employees to do the right things at the right time in the right way. To have an effective management process, it is critical that you have an understanding of the variables that affect performance. Getting and keeping followers occupied in meaningful activity is essential to a leader.

The Basics of Follower Behavior

Much of what is common knowledge about leadership is, in fact, fallacious. Ideas extracted from our experience or that of others may not actually identify the critical variables that made that approach work in that specific situation. We are all taught, for instance, to lead by example and to communicate, communicate, communicate! This kind of advice peddles the banal as wisdom and ignores the essentials.

While the leader's actions and the visual images he or she paints with words are important, these are not the most powerful influences on behavior. Much more has been modeled and communicated than has been done. Simply put, the impact of your example and of your communications is to get followers to do something once, perhaps twice. After that, they must see some personal benefit from their actions or the response to your example and your communications will diminish.

This relationship is clearly stated in the most basic expression of the causes of behavior presented below as the ABC Model.

ANTECEDENT: BEHAVIOR ⟶ CONSEQUENCE

This model shows that there are only two ways to change behavior; by what happens before a behavior and what happens after it. An antecedent is simply anything that tells you what to do. It could be a memo, a meeting, company policy, this book, or a thousand things that we see, hear, touch, smell, or taste in a day. In most cases, the antecedent contains enough information for us to know exactly what to do. However, knowing what to do and doing it are two different things. The telephone may ring, but because we are in a hurry, we ignore it; we may know a company policy and not follow it; we may know a safety rule but violate it every day; we may know the speed limit and the consequences for speeding, but exceed it every day. All of these things point to the fact that most problems that organizations face daily are not the result of not knowing what to do but are often treated by the organization as though they are. Most attempts to resolve performance issues involve emphasizing the importance of the actions, stressing the cost of failure, making our expectations clear, re-telling them, creating new policies and procedures, re-training employees and simply nagging them to do the right thing.

Is it possible to train people to do the safe thing or the quality thing and have them do what you trained them to do every time? Can you communicate priorities and have employees make decisions about their time accordingly? Can you delegate to others and know that you will not have to worry about the cost, quality, timeliness, or appropriateness of their actions? Of course, you can.

However, the determinant of whether these things will be done is not the clarity of communication and effectiveness of training, but what happens to employees when they do what has been communicated. If a person was trained to do something one way and when he applied it found that it didn't work, would he continue? If a person is given a priority assignment and then someone comes in with an emergency request, will the priority likely be put aside? If a person is delegated responsibility for a project and the boss second-guesses every action that the person takes, will the person soon defer all decisions to the boss? You know the answer to these types of questions.

Leaders who think that people will do their best because that's what is expected of them are prone to make errors by relying primarily on antecedents. This is especially pernicious because it leads to leadership beliefs and practices that produce suboptimal responses from the followers. You can best understand this when you consider the most important aspect of human behavior.

Behavior is a Function of its Consequences

The closest thing we have to a behavioral law, as gravity is a physical law, is that behavior is a function of its consequences. Antecedents get their power from the consequences that are associated with them. *The bottom line is that the effectiveness of most of what leaders do is determined by how they use behavioral consequences.* We believe if this simple statement was fully understood and put into practice that not a major organization exists that could not improve by 20-30% per year (the government by more than 50%). This law means that *every change* must start with an analysis of what will happen to the performers if they do what we need and what will happen to them if they don't. While most leaders feel that consequences in an organization are in place for those who do or don't do what is required, the consequences that are typically used are often ineffective in either maintaining desirable action or in stopping undesirable action.

Unfortunately, not all consequences are created equal. Some are more effective than others. Most of the consequences that organizations use, such as compensation, performance appraisal, and reward and recognition practices are weak when it comes to getting behavior to occur every day. Despite the common belief that the bigger the reward, the more it impacts behavior, science tells us that the most effective consequences are those that are immediate and certain. The least effective are those that are delayed and uncertain. Guess which category is the most common in the modern organization? Bonuses, profit sharing, promotions, and raises in pay are all positive, but they are future and uncertain consequences to the performers and as such they have little impact on behavior on a day-to-day basis. The size of the payoff only increases the pool of people who want to participate in the activity and has little to say about how well they will work once selected.

Things that save your followers time and effort are almost always positive, immediate, and certain. Problem solving requires a disciplined approach, for instance, because the reinforcers for most people come from solving the problem, not from analyzing the causes of the problem. Bypassing the analysis phase allows them to get into action sooner so that they experience immediate, positive consequences sooner and more often.

A common leadership issue is the execution of strategy. Every day, opportunities for positive, immediate, and certain consequences arise for less consequential behaviors which compete with the leader's strategy. If the leader's process for implementing his strategy doesn't have built-in positive, immediate, and certain consequences (PICs), then such consequences must be created to keep the implementation plan on schedule.

The leader must ensure that the followers are receiving PICs on a daily basis. If they are not built into the business processes (which they rarely are), the leader must find a way to overlay them onto the process. One of the ways leaders do this is by taking work out of the process. This is a common task where the leader runs interference for the follower and removes obstacles wherever possible rather than requiring the follower to surmount each obstacle unaided. In this way the leader reduces the number of negative, immediate, and certain consequences (NICs) experienced by the followers.

While important, removing an obstacle to performance (NIC) does not guarantee that the desired performance will take place. A client of Aubrey Daniels International (ADI), a midwest bank, discovered this truism after they spent millions of dollars removing certain types of paperwork from their branches. Their consultants had convinced them that the administrative burden was suppressing sales. To increase sales, paperwork was reduced by 90%, yet sales didn't increase. They failed by not building-in PICs for the new behaviors, a very common mistake. They built-in bonuses thinking that doing so would drive the correct behavior. Bonuses are positive, future, and uncertain consequences (PFUs) from the performers' perspective and are weak performance drivers.

You will avoid these kinds of failures if you examine in detail the behaviors you are asking for prior to implementing your plan. What happens to the individual when she does what you expect? We find the best answers to that question when we perform what we call a PIC/NIC Analysis®, (see Figure 11.1), which is often very revealing when planning any organizational change.

Figure 11.1 Implementing Six Sigma

ANTECEDENT	BEHAVIOR	CONSEQUENCE	P/N	I/F	C/U
Training	Implementing Six Sigma	More Work	N	I	C
Leader priority		Takes time	N	I	C
Benchmarking		Might get recognition	P	F	U
Champions		Might get criticized	N	I/F	U
		Other work not done	N	I	C

Figure 11.2 (below) shows the relative effect of the various consequence combinations. Note that PICs and NICs are the most effective. Of
course PICs are the most effective in increasing effort whereas NICs are
the most effective way to stop a behavior. Note also that the least effective
patterns are PFU and NFU, the ones that are the most commonly used in
organizations. We threaten to fire (NFU), promise a promotion (PFU),
reward (PFU), give recognition (PFU), and give bonuses (PFU).

Figure 11.2 Relative Effects of PIC/NIC Consequences

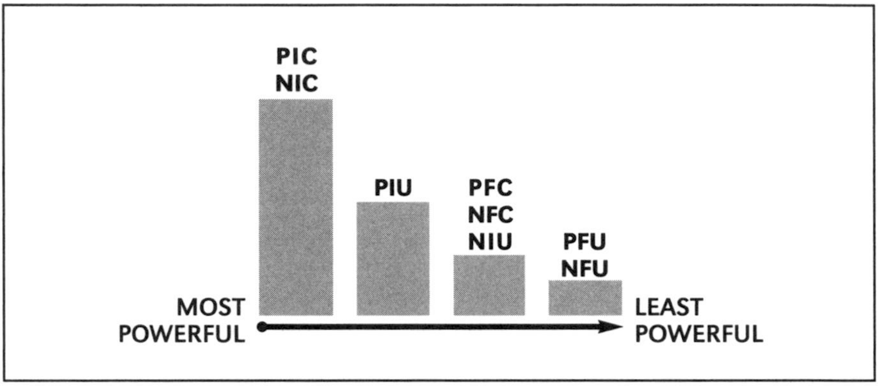

One of our clients had grown significantly by acquiring other
firms. In preparing for the next acquisition, they analyzed some of their
past weaknesses using the PIC/NIC Analysis to identify ways to
improve integrating these acquisitions into their own culture. One key
factor they found was that too many managers tried to impose their
culture on the new employees, in essence telling them how things
would be done as opposed to finding the best way to merge the two
units. Figure 11.3 (on the next page) represents some of their findings
around how they had structured this activity for their own managers.

Armed with this analysis, they changed their plan to provide more
PICs for the behaviors they wanted and to eliminate the PICs they
had found for the undesired behaviors. Their next acquisition, a much
larger one than they had previously attempted, was more successful.

Figure 11.3 Following own culture's procedures rather than merging cultures

ANTECEDENT	BEHAVIOR	CONSEQUENCE	P/N	I/F	C/U
Our culture is successful	Following own culture's procedures rather than merging cultures	Easier	P	I	C
Priority is on making the numbers		Frees more time to spend with our customers	P	I	C
Belief that our culture won't support their new practices		Nothing bad. Not a priority for my boss	P	I	C
		Might lose job	N	F	U
		Might get chewed out	N	F	U
		More culture problems	N	F	U

With any change in an organization, the leader must see to it that immediate positive consequences are available for the new performances in order to realize the benefits of the change. This applies to whether you are trying to change the behavior of an individual or a group, reorganize the company, or merge two diverse cultures. To produce maximum results, PICs must be understood at every level of the organization. The same is true of the marketplace. Competitive advantage goes to those companies that provide the most PICs for the customer. Every process that requires the customer to fill out a form or even wait a few extra seconds for service will lose customers to those companies that have eliminated those hassles. For example, hotels with the easiest check-in procedures will, over time, attract more customers.

Every behavior has consequences that affect the probability of its future recurrence. Some consequences increase behavior and some decrease behavior. Think about this: Everyone at work engages in thousands of behaviors every working day. Each behavior is either increasing or decreasing in frequency as a result of what happens when the person engages in that behavior. This means that at the end of every working day, people leave the workplace either more excited or less excited about coming to work again tomorrow. Do you, as a leader, know which consequences the members of your workforce are experiencing? Do you know which behaviors are increasing and which are decreasing? How do you make sure that value-adding behaviors are receiving consequences that will increase their frequency and those that don't add value receive consequences that stop them from reoccurring?

Most of the consequences that people receive every day occur naturally. That is, they occur as people interact with the environment. Any behavior that produces a desired effect on the environment will increase. In other words, if something works for you, you will repeat it under similar circumstances. If it doesn't work, you will be less likely to try it again. This occurs when you click a computer mouse and a window opens up on your computer screen or when you push a button on an automobile remote and the car doors unlock. These devices create a consequence that supports the correct behavior so that no additional consequence is necessary.

But behavior, to the performer, is neither good nor bad. It is simply something that works or that does not work for him. Consider a waiter or waitress who is rude to a diner but the customer leaves a tip anyway. In that case the natural consequence inadvertently increased the probability of rude behavior in the future. In the same way, some leaders learn rude, uncompromising, or emotional behaviors in dealing with their followers. They are taught these maladaptive behaviors by followers who respond immediately to inappropriate leader outbursts. Such inadvertent consequences ultimately diminish the ability to lead, but the immediate response by the followers obscures this distant outcome. Effective leaders know that they must be disciplined in their own behavior and not succumb to the subtle follower responses that lead them to be less effective. For the same reasons, leaders recognize that they must create a process that provides the right consequences for follower behavior so that they maintain their focus on the leader's priorities. They do this in one of two ways. First, they build the right consequences into the process. Second, if they can't build them in, they have to create them by other means, usually delivering them in person.

In either case, a precise understanding of behavioral consequences is necessary.

The Behavioral Consequences

There are four behavioral consequences. Two increase behavior and two decrease behavior. If you know the direction of behavior change that is needed, you have a simple choice. If you want more of a behavior, you can either provide positive reinforcement or negative reinforcement. If you want less of a behavior, you simply choose between punishment and penalty. See Figure 11.4.

Figure 11.4 The Four Behavioral Consequences and Their Effects

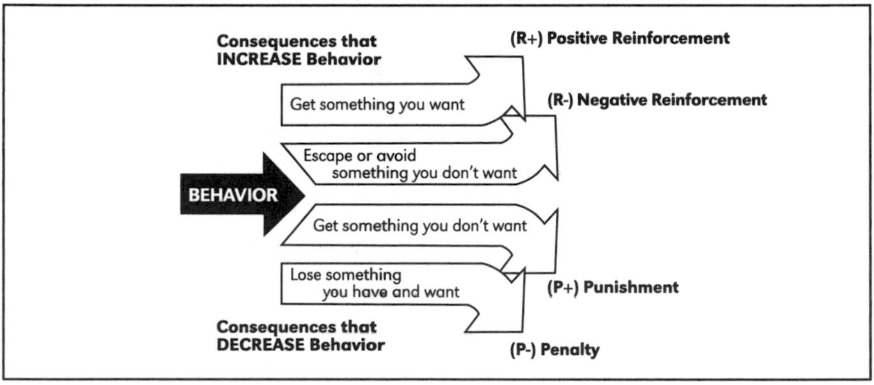

The question often arises that, if both positive and negative reinforcement increase performance, why worry about which to use? To understand the difference between the two consequences, a more technical definition is necessary. Positive reinforcement occurs when a behavior is followed by a consequence that increases its frequency. Negative reinforcement occurs when a person increases a behavior in order to escape or avoid punishment. Careful consideration of these definitions will reveal that under positive reinforcement the upside performance is unlimited. As long as the reinforcer is available and effective, it will cause performance to continue to increase to its physical asymptote. On the other hand, with negative reinforcement, improvement is limited to the amount of behavior that will terminate or avoid a punisher.

If a goal setting process is driven by negative reinforcement (the vast majority are), improvement will be limited to goal attainment plus enough to ensure avoiding the wrath of the manager. Positive reinforcement is the preferred consequence in business, not just because it is positive, but because it is the only one that creates discretionary effort. Under negative reinforcement, incremental improvement that requires lots of effort is the usual result. In addition, negative reinforcement has several undesirable side effects. When negative reinforcement is the dominant consequence used by management, for instance, absenteeism and turnover go up, shifting blame and hiding errors are common, complaining increases, and morale goes down.

Major General John Schofield understood the problems and dangers of management by negative reinforcement when, in an address to the Corps of Cadets at West Point, he said the following:

> The discipline which makes the soldiers of a free country reliable in battle is not to be gained by harsh or tyrannical treatment. On the contrary, such treatment is far more likely to destroy than to make an army. It is possible to impart instruction and to give commands in such a manner and such a tone of voice to inspire in the soldier no feeling but an intense desire to obey, while the opposite manner and tone of voice cannot fail to excite strong resentment and a desire to disobey. The one mode or the other of dealing with subordinates springs from a corresponding spirit in the breast of the commander. He who feels the respect which is due to others cannot fail to inspire in them regard for himself, while he who feels, and hence manifests, disrespect toward others, especially his inferiors, cannot fail to inspire hatred against himself (Schofield, 1879).

Most leaders and managers who use negative reinforcement don't know that they do because they don't see themselves as using harsh or tyrannical treatment. However, in today's workplace, negative reinforcement is by far the more prevalent management method. There are two primary reasons for this. First, employees who are managed by negative reinforcement won't tell their supervisors because they are afraid they will shoot the messenger. As most readers of this book know, some employees will not even tell their real opinions on morale surveys because they are afraid their answers will not be truly anonymous. Second, a manager may think that because she has very few negative interactions with employees that she is not a negative reinforcer. We know many very nice people who are almost totally negatively reinforcing managers because their neglect of positive reinforcement constitutes negative reinforcement in the workplace. If, as a leader, you are not actively providing positive reinforcement, you are by definition using negative reinforcement to get things done (Daniels, 2000; Daniels and Daniels, 2004).

It must be pointed out that behavioral consequences are neither good nor bad in and of themselves. They simply produce a predictable response. Depending on the response that is desired or necessary, any of the four may be appropriate. If the behavior needs to stop immediately, as in matters of ethical and safety violations, punishment is the consequence to use. If we have no behavior to positively reinforce, we may need to use a negative reinforcement contingency to get one. In any ongoing relationship, at work or at home, occasions will arise for which any of the four consequences may be appropriate. It is not the type of consequence that is the problem, but the frequency of its use. In any productive relationship, however, the use of consequences other than positive reinforcement should decrease over time.

Positive Reinforcement

There is little doubt scientifically that positive reinforcement is the most powerful interpersonal tool available to people in any relationship. Yet, at the same time, it is the most misunderstood and misused of all the consequences. Business books have consistently trivialized the concept. It is difficult for executives to take one-minute praisings, warm fuzzies, and atta-boys seriously when they are charged with difficult decisions about the bottom line. Of course, it is our contention that if leaders are responsible for the bottom line, the thing they should know the most about is positive reinforcement as it is the only consequence that can maximize all aspects of the corporation's performance.

The value of being positive has been taught in business for well over a half century. Dale Carnegie wrote *How to Win Friends and Influence People* in 1936. His book is still in print, and his advice is still valuable today. However, Carnegie did not have the advantage of the last half century of research on human behavior. What we have learned since 1936 is that positive reinforcement can be used to create or to destroy performance. Because of its power, seemingly minor changes in what is done, how it is done, and the frequency with which it is delivered cannot only cause failure, it can even lead to disastrous results. We don't often think of terrorist acts as occurring as a result of positive reinforcement, but they are. Just as surely as they increase over time, the terrorists are receiving positive reinforcement for their terroristic acts. Journalists are quick to report the group that claimed responsibility and to publish their faces and names all over the news and thereby, inadvertently, give terrorists positive reinforcement.

The worst advice you can give to another is to *always be positive.* As noted, in some situations it is in the best interest of the other person to be told no. We have been in many plants where the advice given to managers and supervisors following a poor morale survey was to be more positive. As we were told by a plant manager, "Employees here don't appreciate a thing you do for them. Every year when we get the morale survey results, I tell these supervisors and managers, 'Don't you let the sun set on your back until you fix everything you can fix on this survey.'" He then pulled out a chart showing percent favorable ratings on the survey and those ratings were dropping like a rock. "We have spent over two million dollars in the last three years trying to please people by improving things in this plant and this is the thanks we get. We can't please 'em no matter how hard we try."

What this manager didn't understand is a basic rule of behavior— you get more of what you reinforce. It wasn't that he did the wrong things but his timing was bad. By responding directly to complaints, he got more of them. It is unfortunate that his experience taught him that

1) people don't appreciate the good things you do for them, and 2) that you can never please them. Those two things are not true of people as a whole. But because he responded to complaints in such a tangible and visible way, he was inadvertently teaching employees that the best way to get what they wanted was to complain and be continuously dissatisfied.

Leaders should know five things about positive reinforcement:

1. Positive reinforcers are highly personal.

   What is positively reinforcing to one person is not necessarily reinforcing to another. There is no *one size fits all* when it comes to positive reinforcement. Any time you do something across the organization as an attempt at positive reinforcement, expect that some people will not be happy with it. Knowing what each person wants, desires, and will work hard to get is the key to developing successful relationships.

2. Positive reinforcement must be earned.

   Since positive reinforcement strengthens the behavior that precedes it, if it is delivered during or contingent on some valuable work behavior or accomplishment, that behavior is what you will get more of in the future. Increasingly, benefits and other perks are given to everyone contingent only on employment. In both cases the funds expended will pay minimal dividends to the organization because they fall on the good and the poor performers alike. Eisenberger (1989) states in his book, *Blue Monday,* ". . . providing success without effort kills industriousness. In our research we have repeatedly found that rewarded low effort fails to improve performance on subsequent tasks." The leader's job is to make sure that policies, processes, and management behaviors create conditions where employees actually earn positive reinforcement.

3. Positive reinforcement must be frequent.

   One positive reinforcer doesn't make a habit. To get people to work at their best requires reinforcement every day. Leaders must find ways to build positive reinforcement into work processes and work relationships if maximum results are to be achieved. Any system or process that limits how many people receive reinforcement presents a problem. For example, if your performance appraisal system limits the number or percentage of people who can get the top rating, you will create employees who are apathetic toward the system. Or, if they care about the rating, it will likely induce unhealthy competition. Either outcome is bad for the organization. Employees should not have to compete with each other for reinforcement. Employee of the Month and other programs that involve public ranking of employees should be avoided. There are easier ways to upset people. Getting people to the point where giving their best is an effortless habit requires hundreds of reinforcers, not an occasional pat on the back. Creating the workplace where this is commonplace is a task for real leaders.

4. Positive reinforcement should be immediate.

   Positive reinforcers reinforce the behavior that is occurring at the time the performer receives the reinforcer. Delay of reinforcement, recognition, and reward are almost always problematic because they are likely to increase behavior other than the particular behavior you want repeated. The best time to deliver positive reinforcement is when people are engaged in the behavior that you want or like. Therefore all positive reinforcement is a PIC!

5. The best positive reinforcers are not financial.

   Because of the frequency necessary to attain and maintain high-and-steady rate performance, it should be obvious that financial reinforcers cannot be the mainstay of any efficient and effective work environment. Good personal relationships are the source of the best reinforcement. Social reinforcers such as positive comments on reports or graphs, a demonstration of interest in someone's work or anything that lets a person know that you like, value, or appreciate their work or accomplishments, cost little or nothing and when done appropriately cannot be given too often. Tangibles (financial) are used occasionally to back up social reinforcers (Daniels and Daniels, 2004).

A large part of the leader's role in creating the best working environment is to make sure that positive reinforcement is understood and delivered for the right behaviors, at the right time, and at the right frequency. *This means that all policies and procedures should be examined from this perspective.* It is folly to reinforce one behavior and expect another, but it happens in organizations every day. To avoid this, review policies, procedures, and initiatives frequently.

Withholding Positive Reinforcement

When a behavior has been increased through positive reinforcement, and the reinforcement is discontinued for some reason, the behavior will eventually return to its pre-reinforcement level. The technical term for this return to baseline levels is *extinction*. This is how organizations most commonly lose the discretionary behavior of their people.

Most extinction in organizations is unplanned. When your followers engage in extra effort and it goes unappreciated, that extra effort will stop rather quickly. Extinction is the cause of most of the loss of excitement and enthusiasm for organizational initiatives. Because most initiatives involve some positive reinforcement for those who like to do new things, they are energized by the learning and newness involved in the change. Once the learning has occurred and the newness has worn off, the enthusiasm and excitement dies, not a natural death as most believe, but as the result of the loss of reinforcement.

Sometimes, extinction can be used deliberately to stop unwanted behavior. When people do unnecessary or undesired things primarily for the purpose of getting your attention, the best thing you can do is to ignore that behavior. When you do, however, expect that the behavior will get worse before it gets better. Such an increase in behavior is called an *extinction burst*. Frequently, a leader who doesn't understand extinction will respond to an extinction burst, making the problem much worse than it was in the beginning. Businesses have been victims of this phenomenon for the last hundred years when negotiating with labor. Not getting what they want, labor may resort to various threats and even violence in some cases. And just at that time, management reaches a settlement. When unions become ever more difficult to deal with, management has only itself to blame.

As you understand the power of positive reinforcement in human affairs, you begin to see that it should not be taken lightly. You are changing behavior regardless of what you do. As a leader you need to understand how consequences are being used in your workplace so that you can optimize your leadership effectiveness.

In the final analysis, creating the right conditions for discretionary behavior is the responsibility of the leader. While the leader does not have to personally deliver positive reinforcement to all the followers, the systems, policies, processes, and skills of managers and followers should be developed to facilitate its efficient and effective delivery.

chapter 12

ADDING MEANING TO THE FOLLOWER'S WORK

The greatest leader is not one who does great things.

He's the one who gets people to do great things.

President Ronald Reagan

Creating meaningful change is at the heart of leadership. The obvious change that leaders are often called on to make is to radically transform an organization through downsizing, re-engineering, mergers and acquisitions, or through some other highly visible activity or result. However, the more common change is that which occurs every day where people discover and implement more efficient and effective ways of improving the organization. In any event, if change is not seen as meaningful, little or no discretionary effort will be directed toward it. As discussed earlier, without discretionary effort, leaders usually fail.

Creating Meaningful Work

Before discussing the leader's role in changing the organization, let's consider the manager's role in creating meaningful work. Most attempts to create meaningful work have focused on altering the job. Volvo was among the most publicized companies to make such an attempt in the 1960s. They had an assembly-line system where the employee who formerly just put on a door, now did many more things to the car. It was thought that job enrichment, the opposite of work simplification, would increase motivation, quality, and pride. Unfortunately, the benefits attained by these new methods were short-lived.

Meaningful work is not determined by what people do but rather by what happens to them when they do it. The way to create meaningful work, therefore, is not to change the activity, but to change the consequences for engaging in the activity. Many people do simple activities as often as possible that provide them with considerable satisfaction. If you examine the behavior of playing a slot machine in a casino, for instance, it would certainly not, at first glance, appear to be stimulating or exciting. The behaviors are basically putting a coin in the machine and pulling a handle or pushing a button. However, people can become addicted to it. For many people, the anticipation of playing adds meaning to their weekend. These same behaviors in the workplace—putting raw material into a machine and pulling a handle or pushing a button to activate a metal press—are viewed as boring and monotonous. The way these jobs are typically structured causes managers to have to deal with problems of employee burnout, low performance, absenteeism, and turnover.

To make any activity meaningful you have to provide consequences that are meaningful to the performer. Although the critic will point out that pulling the handle of a slot machine sometimes produces money, we must point out that although a few people win in the short run, none win if they continue to play. Many repetitive activities, particularly in sport and leisure, define people's lives. Money is usually not their motivator in these activities.

In an appliance manufacturing plant, for example, one job was very much like the slot machine example. The performer had to place a blank metal disc in a jig, operate a lever, remove the stamped part, and place it in a container. An older employee who had been doing this job for many years actually produced more parts than several automatic machines that made similar parts. The secret was in the fact that her machine was located near the supervisors' office. As they passed her machine, without exception, each one would pick up the container, rattle it, and make some positive comment about how many she could do. Although she was senior enough to have changed jobs over the years, she didn't because of the tremendous amount of reinforcement she received for her performance from managers, visitors, and peers.

Effective positive reinforcement creates meaningful work. It is a leader's responsibility to make sure that it exists for all work. Employee benefits and money are the most common ways that executives attempt to provide positive reinforcement for good work, but for a variety of reasons such perks are not effective in creating the kind of discretionary effort that leaders need (Abernathy, 1996; Daniels, 2000).

Creating Reinforcers for Change

The real challenge of leadership is to connect meaningful work with meaningful change. If you have an organization where people are engaged in meaningful work, change is relatively easy to accomplish. Implicit in this is that people feel a part of something bigger than their immediate activity. Many occupations by their very nature attract people who want to be associated with the organizational mission and vision. NASA attracts a lot of people who want to be associated with the space program because of the adventure, technical challenges, and the general awe with which the public holds their activities. The entertainment industry is the same. Many young people are attracted to politics because they want to be a part of making the country a better place. It is easy to see why people would be drawn to such jobs. It is also easy to understand why people will put up with inept managers and management by negative reinforcement in these jobs. The mission creates reinforcers for the performers.

Being a leader in a glamorous industry is easier than in one considered mundane. The question arises for most leaders, "What can I do, because my organization is not in a glamour industry?" Over the years we have seen many people who had jobs loading trucks, working as janitors, clerks, and factory workers who felt the same about their organization as the engineers in NASA. If you understand how to create positive reinforcers, the industry or the job doesn't matter.

The Establishing Operation

An important concept in behavior analysis is called the *establishing operation (EO)*. An establishing operation is "any change in the environment which alters the effectiveness of some object or event as reinforcement and simultaneously alters the momentary frequency of the behavior that has been followed by that reinforcement" (Michael, 1982).

You may love Coca Cola but you do not get a Coke from every Coke machine that you pass. On the other hand, a friend says, "How about a Coke?" You may say, "O.K." The friend's question is an EO for drinking a Coke. While the mere availability did not prompt you to want one, the prospect of drinking a Coke with a friend made the drink more appealing.

The point is that nothing is always positively reinforcing. A drink of water is highly sought when you are hot and thirsty, but after quenching your thirst, it is no longer motivating. Although Bruster's White Turtle ice cream is great, after eating their huge double scoop on a waffle cone, only the rare person would want a second helping. To say to that person, even a child, at that point, "If you will do X, I will buy you another ice cream," would probably cause her to laugh. Ice cream would be a poor motivator at that time. Satiation decreases the value of a reinforcer. Deprivation increases it. Therefore, one way to create reinforcers is to limit the amount of reinforcement available. Diamonds owe much of their value to the fact that they are perceived to be scarce. Diamond producers are said to limit the quantity of diamonds for sale each year as a means of keeping the price high.

However, making reinforcers scarce is not really an option for a leader. Remember, reinforcers affect behavior only after they are received. The scarcer they are, the fewer people are affected. Employee of the Month, Salesman of the Year, and other such programs owe their ineffectiveness to the fact that very few people ever get them or to the fact that, over time, everybody gets them. Whenever an organization limits the number of followers who earn certain reinforcers, morale and performance is diminished.

Leaders are often required to create reinforcers where they normally would not exist. Why would an employee get excited about an organization's mission or vision? Why would employees get excited about reducing costs or eliminating jobs?

Fortunately for leaders, scarcity is not the only way to create reinforcers. If someone is a source of significant positive reinforcement to you, that person can get you to do things that others would not. In a restaurant a woman asked the waiter, "Does your soufflé have nuts in it?" The waiter responded that it did. She said, "I don't like it with nuts; I'll have something else." Her companion said, "Have you ever had the soufflé here?" "No," she replied. "Try it. You will love it. It's terrific!" She turned to the waiter and said, "I'll try it." It was obvious that this was not the first time such a conversation had occurred with this couple. She had some confidence in the fact that he knew her positive reinforcers and punishers. She deferred to his authority because he had not led her astray in the past and she had confidence that he had no motivation to do so now. The leader who is trusted and respected will get people to do things just because he wants them to and because he has a history of consistent pairing of messages with the promised consequences.

People are rarely excited about reducing costs, getting to Six Sigma or reaching organizational objectives, but when the leader understands the EO, a routine task can become something that people will come early and stay late to do. It is through the use of EOs that a leader can make something ordinary into something valuable.

Leaders Connect

The leader has to create an EO for everybody. It is not unusual to find that the leader's initiatives failed even though they connected with front-line employees, because they left middle managers out. An organization's initiatives usually rot from the middle. Leaders must make sure that any new initiative has benefits to all levels of management and staff. Like middle children, the middle managers are frequently forgotten or get most of the work, most of the punishment, and none of the credit if and when an initiative is successful. Peters and Waterman's *In Search of Excellence* (1982), concept of MBWA (Management By Walking Around) turned out to be, in a large number of cases, a punisher to middle managers. The executive who did the walking around saw problems on the floor and then blamed the supervisors or managers.

A distribution VP, anticipating an impending downsizing, developed a program called Step-Up. The program was designed to reward people for figuring out a way to eliminate work. If an employee could figure out a way to eliminate his job, he would be given a higher paying job somewhere else in the company or would be given an equal paying job with a bonus equal to 10% of the annual salary for the old job. In the first week, several people stepped forward to show how their jobs could be eliminated. For the next several weeks no one else did so. While one might think that no one else could think of a way to eliminate a job, that was not the case. When we interviewed employees, we found that they were being punished for talking about ways to eliminate jobs. The reason was that when the early volunteers stepped up, their supervisors were punished by their managers. Earlier the supervisors had been asked to cut out all the unnecessary work in their areas and when their employees figured out a way to eliminate work, their supervisors were punished for not knowing that was possible. Managers punished supervisors. Supervisors punished employees. The initiative fell far short of its potential. If one person's success means punishment for others within the same unit, you should anticipate dissension and failure.

An engineer in a chemical plant in Texas said, "We are getting too many ideas. It costs us about $125 to process an idea. And most of them are not worth that. So we have decided that next year we are not going to fool with an idea that we think is not worth more than $125." That will work! If this engineer wants fewer ideas, that move will certainly do the trick. A fact that upper management should know is that someone who has an idea today that is worth $10 and is positively reinforced for thinking about how to do a job better, may have a multimillion dollar idea tomorrow. However, if you don't seriously consider $10 ideas, you will rarely see the multimillion dollar kind. It is important to understand that the problem here is not with the engineer. The problem is in the process that was created to handle ideas. The president of the company was continually asking employees to "share your ideas, any ideas, with us." But the system that was created resulted in more work for the engineers. Processing new ideas for this engineer was extra work, and not something that would make a substantial difference in his performance evaluation. As a matter of fact, if he spent too much time investigating new ideas, his primary job might suffer and his performance evaluation would probably reflect it.

Before any leader stands before a group to tell about some new initiative, that leader must make sure that everyone is connected in a meaningful way. Certainly you want managers and supervisors to be on a crusade for your cause. That will not happen if reinforcement and punishment contingencies are not aligned from the top to the bottom.

Leaders Have a Vision

More organizational time and resources have been wasted on mission, vision, and values than any other initiative. Most went into it because it was the thing to do and we might add, in our opinion, many consultants who led the activity didn't understand the process either.

A mission is important only to determine the definition of success. A mission can be for a job or an organization, but of course, is not the same for both. Most mission statements are too long and exist more for display on the wall of the reception room and on Web pages instead of fulfilling the practical purpose of serving as a guide to performance on a daily basis. Will Potter, mentioned earlier, was famous in his company for approaching employees and asking them how what they were doing was helping Preston meet its mission. If they could tell him, which almost all could, he would usually treat them to a break or a meal.

The vision is a statement of why the mission is important. Ideally, it should be inspirational and create some emotion in the employee. GE's vision is "We bring good things to life." Dupont's is "Better living through chemistry." ADM's is "The technology of feeding a growing world." Other visions that we have seen are "Fighting hunger," "Cleaning up our planet," "Preventing disease," and "Nature has solutions." In the movie, *The Blues Brothers,* the vision that got the band back together after the leader had been in prison for several years was "One last gig for the Lord."

A good vision will rally people. For example, in one scene of the movie *Trading Places,* Dan Ackroyd and Eddie Murphy are about to go onto the stock exchange floor to reap revenge on the characters played by Don Ameche and Ralph Bellamy. When Dan turned to Eddie and said, "Let's go kick some butt!" the movie audience routinely broke into a spontaneous cheer. The statement captured the spirit of the crowd. Unfortunately, some statements can stir up such emotion that they provoke riots and other mass actions that seem spontaneous, but they are rooted in previously unnoticed reinforcement histories that include enjoying getting back at authority.

A word of caution about the inspirational and emotional aspects of vision. It is relatively easy to get a group of people fired up about some activity or accomplishment. The emotion generated by a group meeting can elicit commitments from people to act. The real test of an effective vision is what they do after making the commitment. An old story tells of a man who falls off a cliff and is hanging tenaciously to a small tree that is growing out of a rock 1000 feet above the valley floor. Gathering his wits about him, he yells to the cliff above, "Anybody up there?" Receiving no response, he yells at the top of his lungs, "Is there *anybody* up there?" About that time the clouds part and a booming voice comes out of the clouds, "I am here." "Can you help me?" the man pleads. "I can save you if you only believe." The voice responds. "I believe, I believe," the man yells. "Turn loose of that branch and you'll be saved." The man looks down and can hardly see the trees in the valley below. He looks back up and yells, "Is there anybody else up there?"

The point of this story is that you can only tell if people are engaged in a meaningful way by their actions, not by their words. While one would think that leaders don't need to be told this, it is amazing how many times executives judge the success of an initiative, early on, by what people say about it rather than what they do about it. An organization's vision is a call to *action*. The lag between verbal reaction and action is a measure of the initiative's ultimate success. If people are saying your initiative is a good thing, but they just haven't had time to get to it, the effort will not survive. Nail the lid on the coffin.

The evangelist Billy Graham learned early that is was relatively easy to get people at his Crusades to make a public commitment to change their lives. The hard part was to make it stick. What he did was begin to develop the environment that would support the commitment after he was gone. His team worked with local churches months in advance of his Crusade on how to respond to those who came forward during his meetings. We have seen many initiatives where more time was spent on the roll-out than on the implementation. Of course, most of them failed or had a short lifespan. Managers take heed. Farmers don't sow seeds before the ground is prepared. Leaders should not announce a change until they have made sure that from the first day of the change all employees will be positively motivated to take action.

Leaders Deliver

Even if you possess wonderful oratorical skills, you cannot be an effective EO for any mission or vision if the followers don't like you. Mildred Ramsey, a motivational speaker who worked most of her life as a weaver in a textile plant, tells a story of her young supervisor who called her work group together following a management meeting and said, "They told me in the management meeting today that if we don't improve our quality, they are going to run me off." Mildred replied, "We don't care if they run you off." Followers will only care for you if they perceive that you care for them. Unless they care for you, your ability to deliver results by motivating your followers will be limited at best.

Effective leaders must have a history of delivering on their promises. Unfortunately, many people in leadership positions adhere to the old advertising slogan of Arpege perfume, "Promise her anything, but give her Arpege." The employees never even get the Arpege! Politicians are generally held in low regard because they are better at explaining why they didn't deliver on a campaign promise than they are at honoring it. They generally have a very low correlation between what they promise and what the voters perceive they deliver. When leaders deliver on the majority of what they promise, people will cut them some slack even when some of what they promised didn't happen. But if you follow through on a low percentage of the promises you make, people will not even give you credit for the promises that you do keep.

If a leader is the source of frequent, timely reinforcement for a person or a group of people, then whatever is important to the leader is important to them. When such a leader sees the need for change because of a competitor's actions, a change in the economy, or the need for new technology, followers will abandon longstanding behaviors and processes simply because the leader asks them to do so. The new behavior quickly becomes as meaningful as the old because in both cases followers see themselves as working for the cause that is important to the leader.

chapter 13
CREATING EXCITEMENT FOR THE LEADER'S INITIATIVES

Every man loves what he is good at.

Thomas Shadwell (1679)

Most organizations have few jobs that could be considered exciting, but think of the kind of organization you would have if everyone had a job that they considered valuable and exciting! Such a workplace is possible to attain independent of the actual tasks involved in the job. Whether a job is exciting is not a function of what you do, but what happens to you when you do it. If you look at the behavior of a typical executive, you see that she talks, writes, and reads. Not much more. What is exciting about that? If, on the other hand, you look at what happens to her when she does those things, you get an idea of why she loves her job. She asks an employee about a project and he gives her better than expected results. She holds a meeting to introduce a new initiative and gets an enthusiastic response. She reads a research article and gets an idea for a new product. These are the things that make a job exciting—the consequences.

The leader must make the behaviors of any job related to the organization's vision. How do you make annual objectives exciting? The question more formally asked should be, "How do you make the accomplishment of annual objectives a positive reinforcer?" The answer lies in the leader establishing himself as a reinforcer to the followers. When he does, things that are important to the leader become important to the followers.

Franklin D. Roosevelt established himself as a positive reinforcer to millions of Americans very early in his presidency because he delivered on his campaign promises and as such he rallied people to causes he desired. During his candidacy, he promised people a new deal and delivered it in the first hundred days of his presidency.

The week following his inauguration in 1933, he called the Congress into a special session to enact legislation to help overcome the Depression. The legislation included emergency banking laws, new regulations for the securities and insurance industries, establishment of a civilian conservation corps to put a quarter of a million young unemployed workers to work on public projects, and the Agriculture Adjustment Act that gave the federal government extraordinary powers to assist farmers.

During his presidency, Roosevelt's many achievements included unemployment insurance, the National Recovery Administration (formed to enforce codes of conduct within industry while relaxing antitrust laws in order to promote business growth); the Tennessee Valley Authority (the first publicly held utility corporation); the Public Works Administration (which provided funding for infrastructures such as dams, thus creating more jobs), and the National Housing Act (which provided insurance for mortgages).

His accomplishments produced something for almost everyone. He enjoyed tremendous popular support even though he was often opposed by certain segments of the business and industrial community.

His fireside chats on the radio were listened to religiously by millions of people. As a result, he is the only President to be elected for four consecutive terms. Even though he made a campaign promise not to send American troops to fight any foreign wars, he committed American troops to fight the German Navy in the Atlantic Ocean less than one year later. Because he thought it was the right thing to do, people rallied behind him in a way unparalleled in American history. The causes that were important to him became a priority to almost all Americans.

Excitement Resides in Behavioral Consequences

Whether in sports or entertainment, it is not behaviors that create excitement, but the things that happen to the athletes or movie stars that determine continued excitement for the work. Movie stars often arise at 4:00 a.m., sit for several hours in the makeup department, often wearing hot and cramped costumes, and then spend the day in the heat or cold. Athletes spend much time engaging in very repetitive behavior such as drills and calisthenics. But when you begin to look at what happens to performers and athletes when interacting with fellow actors, directors, coaches, players, and fans you can understand why their jobs are so exciting.

As you know by now, there is only one way to create excitement on the job. You guessed it—positive reinforcement. You certainly cannot punish, penalize, or use negative reinforcement to excite someone. While you may talk someone into excitement, it will evaporate quickly if some form of positive reinforcement is not forthcoming.

In many jobs, positive reinforcement isn't present if you don't plan it. As we have mentioned, one of the best ways to do this is to build positive reinforcement into your work process.

Almost every video game has a system for continuous tracking of performance during the game. Anytime you create a task where people can see some graphic display of progress, you are on the way to creating an exciting job. The most effective cycle of performance feedback is continuous. Many jobs don't allow for continuous feedback, so strive to give feedback in the shortest time possible following performance.

While feedback makes excitement possible, feedback alone doesn't create excitement. Feedback sets up opportunities for frequent positive reinforcement. Just a number or a line on a graph has little motivational value unless it represents progress toward something that is important to the performer. Thus the leader has to establish a relationship between the feedback, the accomplishment, and the reinforcers that are available both for the effort and for the success of the followers. One of the best ways a leader can achieve this is by creating themes for significant initiatives.

Themes Cluster Reinforcement

A theme is a way of helping followers visualize success. It usually involves creating some symbolic representation of the objective and progress toward it. One organization used a painting of Mount Fuji with teams of mountain climbers carrying national flags to represent its race with a Japanese competitor to get a particular product on the market first. The painting was displayed in a public area and the teams' progress up the mountain was updated every week against milestones. It was easy for everyone to relate their unit's performance to the climbers and determine best ways to gain even more advantage. The leader referred to the painting frequently, recognizing the progress and contributions of each team's effort. The effect was significant: the painting focused everyone's efforts and discretionary behaviors on the vision which contributed significantly to the initiative's success.

Eastman Chemicals Company developed a theme of "Make International Business Easy" (MIBE) that involved over 132 teams and more than 1200 people from around the globe. The teams worked on improving customer service between their headquarters in Kingsport, Tennessee, and their non-U.S. sales offices around the world. Each team project was represented by a satellite circling the Eastman Chemical World, and when a project was chosen, a linking-in ceremony was held. Annual celebrations provided a time to share results with everyone who contributed to MIBE's success. The project spanned more than two years and produced tremendous benefits. Communication and cooperation improved dramatically in such things as reducing incomplete orders from a baseline of 44% to less than 2%. Time to receive pricing was cut by two-thirds and technical service requests showed a 23% improvement.

One significant advantage in using themes is that the theme gives followers a common rallying point for participating in reinforcement activities for critical behaviors. Being closer to the action, themes create more timely and accurate reinforcers for the critical actions that drive the initiative to success. By providing the focus for reinforcement and celebration, the leader leverages his efforts in a significant way and almost always accelerates the critical actions called for by his plan. Few leadership tools have the power of themes for unifying the followers around a cause and producing high levels of behavior focused on the goal.

While you can overdo anything, themes included, the judicious use of themes can create an environment of excitement, energy, excellence, and even fun that can be turned into a cultural characteristic of an organization. Themes are not slogans; they are visions that clearly lay out the accomplishment and the rules of engagement. Themes tell the followers how their actions contribute to the organization's success and make it possible for the maximum number of individuals to participate in a meaningful way. Perhaps the most important element is that they create anticipation in the follower for the rewards of success, even when the rewards are not tangible or financial. In short, it shows everyone how to be a winner.

Goals Should be Antecedents for Positive Reinforcement

One of the essential parts of a theme that facilitates this kind of excitement is a goal. Unfortunately, in most organizations goals do not create excitement. Rarely do employees look forward to a goal setting process. Many leaders have tried to create excitement by involving people in setting their own goals. Participation, in and of itself, does not generate enthusiasm or excitement. It is quite possible that someone could participate in setting a goal that they have no reasonable expectation of reaching. Our company worked in a New York sales organization where sales managers spent two months a year setting goals with each salesperson. They set targets for each product for every customer. For the two selling seasons prior to our involvement, they reached 9% of goal the first season and 11.3% the second. While sales volumes were actually quite high, sales reps were not selling what they had planned to sell. Managers were excited about large volume sales whether or not the products sold were those targeted by the sales plan. Consequently, sales plan targets for specific products were rarely met. Sales planning was a colossal waste of time.

Stretch goals, commonly used in organizations, guarantee that participating in goal setting will *not* be positively reinforcing. While stretch goals are very popular, their effect is to demotivate people, especially over time. By setting stretch goals you are effectively reducing the probability of reinforcement. Stretch goals originated because the typical goal setting process is driven by negative reinforcement. As mentioned earlier, negative reinforcement causes performance to stop at goal or shortly thereafter. Stretch goals seemed like an efficient way to get employees to go beyond required performance.

Does this mean that you should not set goals such as Six Sigma does? Absolutely not. However, you cannot lead *by* Six Sigma; you must lead *to* Six Sigma. This is not a semantic difference, but a significant behavioral difference. You lead to Six Sigma by reinforcing progress toward the eventual goal. It is of interest to us that most employees involved in Six Sigma cannot tell you where they are, or where the organization is, on the track toward Six Sigma. Without that information, it is difficult to get employees to maintain excitement about any process.

Stretch and difficult goals have a place in some unique circumstances. They can be used as a way to induce creativity, but that would only be for those occasions when we need breakthrough performance. Even on those occasions, if the management style is not based on positive reinforcement, employees will give up quickly or will be difficult to motivate when breakthroughs do not come early.

Since it is not the goals that motivate but the consequences associated with them, goals should be set such that the probability of reaching them is high. Of course, we realize this flies in the face of tradition. However, it is success and the accompanying consequences that not only cause excitement about the current goal but about future goals as well. Here is a suggestion: set management goals so that the probability of reaching them is equal to 100 minus the level of failure that you are willing to accept. If you are willing to accept a 1% failure, then your goal should be set so that it would be achieved at least 99% of the time. This could be an hourly, daily, or weekly goal. While at first glance this would seem to lead to very slow progress, when you understand that positive reinforcement accelerates behavior, then you will recognize that the achievement of small goals increases momentum. Where stretch or difficult goals decrease momentum over time, setting very reachable goals does the opposite.

ADI worked in an Arizona software engineering company that was over 18 months behind schedule and had been so for almost two years. They had been working seven days a week in an effort to catch up with commitments made to their customers. Employees were tired, angry, and discouraged. The organization turned this dilemma around when they started to measure commitments met. Each engineer was asked to make a commitment to the amount of work he or she would complete the following week. Managers were instructed to accept whatever the engineer said, even if it was considerably below what the manager thought was reasonable. The consequence of meeting weekly commitments was that the employee did not have to work on Saturday and Sunday. Of course, the vice president of the facility had some reservations about the project; if they weren't meeting their goal in seven days, how could they possibly meet the goal in five days? The results were nothing short of phenomenal. In 18 months the employees had not only met their schedules, but their facility was 300% more efficient than the east coast facility.

Small goals do not mean that people do not work hard nor do they mean that little is accomplished. Just as a weightlifter tries to increase his number of exercise sets incrementally by one, when you are already striving for excellence, doing a little bit more produces real growth. This is how you develop the culture of industriousness that Eisenberger (1989) refers to in *Blue Monday*. When individuals decide that the goal is possible and desirable, they make the effort. When they decide that the goal is either impossible or not desirable, they will usually choose to do only those tasks that are demanded of them.

This procedure of setting goals in small increments is consistent with the most powerful technique in teaching anything. That technique is called *shaping*. Technically defined, *shaping* is the "positive reinforcement of successive approximations toward a goal." Shaping defines any movement toward some ultimate goal as a reinforceable movement. Shaping is the critical skill in teaching, parenting, coaching, managing, and leading. Shaping requires that the earliest behaviors toward a goal receive reinforcement, even though the behavior may not resemble the ultimate target in quality, speed, or direction. Behavior is the only requirement for shaping. In labor negotiations, for example, negotiators will often reinforce the behavior of agreeing to meet. And, they may initially accept changes that seem off the mark of the final settlement. However, each point of agreement builds momentum toward a final settlement.

Start where performers are, not where the leader wants them to be. If you are working with someone who is below average in performance, it is a recipe for failure to set the initial goal above average or even at the average. Set the goal where the performance is now plus a little bit and reinforce any improvement. Remember that most learning follows an S-shaped, or what mathematicians call a *positively accelerated learning* curve. Using the S-shape, you set very small goals in the beginning, gradually increase the size of the goals as the performer is successful, and then set smaller and smaller goals as he approaches the final goal. Most people set goals for themselves or others on a straight-line basis from baseline to goal. This is why so many people give up on New Year's resolutions. They set a goal of losing two pounds a week and have typically failed at least by the second week. Most failure to change behavior occurs in the first hours or days of trying to change. By setting very small goals you ensure success and thereby create excitement for the task.

A final note about goal setting is that as a leader you are responsible for the success of the followers. That means in goal setting you may have to reduce goals that followers set for themselves. Because stretch goals have been used for so long, people will set unreasonably challenging goals for themselves even when they know that they probably won't reach them. In that case, the leader must scale them back to a level where success is highly probable.

In summary, excitement and enthusiasm at work is a leader's responsibility. The leader must make sure that the workplace is rich in positive reinforcement. Excitement is not a function of what people do. Even very routine tasks can be made more interesting when the proper amount of positive reinforcement is received for doing it. Graphs that allow for daily tracking of performance and positive reinforcement for improvement are probably the two most powerful techniques a leader can use to create an exciting workplace.

chapter 14

MAINTAINING EXCITEMENT OVER TIME

Nothing great was ever achieved without enthusiasm.

Ralph Waldo Emerson (1841)

Because most organizations' initiatives are undertaken without a conscious change in consequences for the followers, most organizations don't survive. Companies using the techniques described herein have maintained energy and excitement for an initiative for over 25 years.

When we think of excitement, we usually think of a transitory change in mood. Momentary excitement is something we all experience from time to time. Excitement in the workplace, if it occurs at all, is usually infrequent and short-lived. However, in another venue—courtship—almost everyone has had at least one relationship in which they have maintained excitement for long periods of time. Courtship is an example that most people can relate to as lasting for months and sometimes years. Many people maintain excitement about sports for a lifetime. Avid golfers will play in cold, heat, wind, and rain. They will play when they can hardly walk or when arthritis causes them pain when they grip the club. Is it possible for an organization to create this same excitement about its mission, vision, and values? Of course it is.

Excitement defined in behavioral terms is the "anticipation of, or participation in, positive reinforcement." Understanding excitement from this perspective clarifies the leader's role. The effective leader is responsible for creating an environment in which positive reinforcement is a frequent event. How frequent and under what conditions is the subject matter behavior analysts call *schedules of reinforcement* (Daniels, 2004). Dr. Lou Cohen, late dean of clinical psychology at the University of Florida, summarized the study of psychology as involving only two problems: (1) getting a behavior to occur for the first time and (2) getting the behavior to occur again. Leaders want to know how to get behavior to occur again and again and again and again. Fortunately, it is not necessary to understand all the research on schedules of reinforcement to be an effective leader; even though thousands of studies have been conducted over the last 70 years. The reason for studying schedules of reinforcement is that they produce predictable patterns of behavior. Schedules that produce excitement and enthusiasm are the ones associated with intermittent reinforcement.

Two simple classifications for reinforcement schedules are *continuous* and *intermittent.* A continuous schedule of reinforcement is one in which every behavior produces a reinforcer. An intermittent schedule is one in which reinforcement occurs from time to time. Continuous reinforcement is appropriate for a training situation and leads to quick mastery of concepts and skills. Intermittent reinforcement is used to maintain behavior once it reaches a high-and-steady rate (HSR). In most company training, students receive only intermittent reinforcement from the beginning of training. When intermittent reinforcement is used while learning something new, training times are lengthened and performance often does not reach a high-and-steady rate by the end of training. This causes many companies to finish the training on the job. However, when employees receive high rates of reinforcement in the early stages of learning, training times have been cut to a fraction of the standard times and on-the-job performance often exceeds that of more experienced performers within a matter of days. Frequently, salespeople are sent into the field before becoming fluent at product knowledge or the sales process. Compared to the additional cost of training to fluency, the cost of lost sales is enormous.

The answer to the question "How long do I have to do this positive reinforcement?" is answered by another question: "How long do you want the behavior to last?" Without reinforcement, behavior undergoes extinction and eventually stops. This is true of the most self-motivated person you know. The casual observer of behavior usually does not notice that so-called self-motivated people provide reinforcers for themselves when they don't receive it from others. High performers set up reinforcers and rewards for themselves in the absence of such from managers. Of course, all leaders wish that all followers would provide their own motivation because the job of delivering high rates of reinforcement can seem onerous. An interesting paradox: the more frequently people receive reinforcement from you, the less reinforcement they need from you. The extent to which employees are proud of their work accomplishments is highly correlated with the amount of reinforcement they receive from outside sources.

In a previous chapter, we mentioned Eisenberger's (1992) research into what he labeled *learned industriousness*. Eisenberger discovered that positive reinforcement for extra effort produces not only high rates of performance in the reinforced area of work, but that the extra effort is extended to areas of work not directly reinforced by the manager. Frequent reinforcement causes hard work to be satisfying. With the proper reinforcement, people even learn to like difficult and challenging work. In addition, people who are reinforced for extra effort show more ethical and moral behavior than those merely reinforced for task completion. If you are capturing employees' discretionary effort, you are creating followers who are characterized by learned industriousness.

Eisenberger's work has direct and practical applications for leaders. First, the leader needs some system to know who is exerting extra effort. Second, the leader needs some way of getting reinforcement to those people who are exerting extra effort toward the organization's mission and vision, and they should receive reinforcement at a frequency that will keep their behavior and excitement going. We know people who have been applying the techniques described in this book for over 25 years and are just as excited about their work today as they were 25 years ago. Keeping people excited about any kind of work is not an impossible dream.

Earning the Right to Leisurely Leadership

In his classic book *Human Competence,* Gilbert (1996) presents what he calls "leisurely theorems of work." He quotes a Taoist maxim that is particularly relevant to effective leadership: *"Only those who take leisurely what the people of the world are busy about can be busy about what the people of the world take leisurely."* For the leaders who understand the full impact of reinforcement on behavior, there is little need for firefighting and running from task to task with breakneck speed. Since leaders work through others and since positive reinforcement accelerates performance, the well-placed reinforcer can energize the follower to achieve at high levels. An analogy may be helpful.

Most people at some time during their childhood turned their bicycle upside down and spun the front wheel. You may have exerted considerable effort toward getting the wheel to spin as fast as you could. Even though you had to work hard to get maximum spin rate, once there it was relatively easy to maintain the high rate. All you did was occasionally hit the wheel in a spinning motion. You could, in a leisurely manner, keep the wheel spinning indefinitely. Since many leaders only give new behavior or initiatives a lick and a promise in the beginning, it doesn't take long, without reinforcement, for the behavior to stop. This necessitates continually starting over. The key then is 1) invest enough time and effort in the beginning to get the followers to a high-and-steady rate, and 2) reinforce only occasionally once followers have reached this rate of performance; but, be sure to reinforce occasionally or the wheels will eventually stop spinning.

Intermittent reinforcement keeps followers excited and enthusiastic and is the most effective way to help people perform beyond their own expectations. It is a rare person who cannot be motivated to perform at higher rates. We have witnessed many situations in which performers more than doubled their output and declared that they were not working harder. Positive reinforcement makes difficult tasks easier. The extra effort under proper conditions is viewed as an opportunity for satisfaction, rather than a burden.

In the last 30 years of helping people solve problems at work using this technology, many have become enthusiasts for helping others at work, at home, and in their communities. Their successes have kept them excited for a lifetime.

chapter 15

CREATING MOMENTUM

No sooner said than done—so acts your man of worth.

Quintus Ennius (169 B.C.)

Momentum is all about discretionary effort. For leaders, it is about how many of the followers actually spring into action at the leader's request, doing more of what is asked and doing it as quickly as they can. Keep in mind that discretionary effort can only be captured with positive reinforcement. While negative reinforcement will cause people to act, their behavior is directed toward escaping from a negative situation or avoiding some negative interaction. Positive reinforcement has infinitely more value to a leader and the organization than negative reinforcement.

Mass

Since positive reinforcement affects individual behavior, the leader must be concerned with how to deliver reinforcement in such a way that his initiatives, requests, and desires produce reinforcement for the largest number of followers. The first job of leaders, then, is to establish themselves as positive reinforcers. If leaders are not positive reinforcers, they are negative reinforcers by default. In other words, the absence of positive reinforcement for performance is negative reinforcement. Other than producing a culture of doing just enough to get by, negative reinforcement has other more damaging side effects such as resentment of management, apathy toward the work, lack of a sense of urgency, and, eventually, increased absenteeism and turnover. To create a positively reinforcing workplace, the leader has to take the initiative to deliver, or cause to be delivered, frequent positive reinforcement.

In his book, *Coercion and Its Fallout,* Dr. Murray Sidman (1998) points out that people don't have to be taught to be punishers but they most often have to be taught to be positive reinforcers. Leaders are rarely taught to be positive reinforcers, except in the most trivial and simplistic ways. They are told to be positive, give recognition and praise, and to reward outstanding performers. They essentially believe that plaques, trophies, a pat on the back, Employee of the Month awards, and money are the essence of positive reinforcement. Rarely are managers taught that positive reinforcement is really about relationships, not tangible or public acts. If the followers don't like you, there is little chance that your words, written or verbal, or even money and other tangible items that you may deliver will create the results that you desire. If negative reinforcement (often referred to as the *do it or else method*—stated or implied) is the primary way that leaders get things done, they will have little success when they infrequently use praise, recognition, or rewards. In the negatively reinforcing workplace, you cannot turn positive reinforcement on and off like a faucet. As Tom Odom of Shell Oil says, "It's hard to celebrate when you've been beat up on the way to the party." If people don't like you, they will never give you their best.

How then, do you establish yourself as a positive reinforcer?

1. *Do what you say you are going to do.*

   It is good advice for anyone who wants to be a leader to say less and do more. It is particularly important for a leader in a new position not to make promises early, because unforeseen events almost always work to reduce trust rather than increase it. It is often better to announce what you have done rather than communicate what you intend to do. Before making promises, be a student at the feet of the followers.

2. *Be a student.*

   When coming into a new leadership position, or in improving an existing one, the first order of business is to spend some time learning about the followers and what they do. However, you should learn from the followers, not from the numbers or reports of others. Be a student of the follower. Both authors of *Measure of a Leader,* having served in the military, witnessed senior officers who transferred into our units with a variety of management styles. The most common style was that the replacement came into the unit and immediately began making changes and talking about how his previous unit did things in a better way. We can state categorically that these guys never captured discretionary effort. The senior officers who were the best, and those who were sorely missed when they left, were those officers who spent time having the troops show them how they did things and who frequently pointed out the positive attributes of what they learned as they listened to the troops.

   Dr. Judith Komaki, professor of psychology and leadership researcher, has done important behavioral research to uncover critical leadership behaviors. She and her researchers have discovered that the single most important leadership behavior is monitoring. This is not MBWA (Management by Walking Around). The critical attributes are seeking to obtain information, and only information concerned with performance (Komaki, 1998). In her definition, she explicitly defines *monitoring* as inquiry into the relationship between the performer and his work.

A question that you could ask several times a day is, "How did you do that?" The more you ask the question, the quicker you will become a positive reinforcer to those involved in teaching you. No matter the overall condition of a workplace, some things are working well or better than those of your prior experience and people can always teach you valuable things about the organization and its workforce. Your job—find them. At the end of every workday, ask, "What did I learn today and who taught me?" The answers will tell you who you reinforced that day.

3. *Discover the positive reinforcers of the followers.*

If you have been a student of the followers, you already discovered something that is positively reinforcing to almost everyone—teaching or showing you something that they know, can do, or have done. However, that is only a small part of what is reinforcing. Every person has a unique set of positive reinforcers. Fortunately, you do not need to know all of a person's reinforcers to develop an effective working relationship, but you must know some of them. Although some reinforcers have rather broad appeal, they are few. Spend time learning the reinforcers for each person. Nothing is reinforcing to everyone—not money, not sex, not alcohol, and certainly not tee shirts, ball caps or company logo items. To be truly reinforcing and to be most effective, leaders must know the reinforcers of each of their direct reports. Span of control is determined by the number of employees who can be effectively reinforced. This number can be increased or decreased by the extent to which the work environment is designed to produce reinforcers for value-added behavior.

Over the last 30 years of teaching behavioral technology to leaders and managers, the most asked question by far is, "What are some positive reinforcers that I can use?" Of course our answer is, "Only the followers can tell you." They tell you by what they say and by what they do. It is a good habit to keep a list of those things and activities that followers find reinforcing. Make a notebook or a computer file with a page for each performer where you can store and update the information. Get the performer to help you and have a conversation with each person to make sure that the list is current. Remember that we change every day. Something that is reinforcing to someone today may not be six months from now. By the way, many people find it a positive event just to be asked about the things that they like or the activities they enjoy. If people are reluctant to tell you those things that they like or are willing to invest their discretionary time or money to do, it is probably a subtle sign of management by negative reinforcement.

The challenge for the leader is to make sure that all the followers are receiving positive reinforcement for behavior that is directed toward the organization's mission. Obviously, the number of levels of management complicates this aspect of the leader's job. However, research shows that people who receive reinforcement are more likely to reinforce others. Because reinforcement multiplies as it moves through the management chain, a little reinforcement at the top creates considerable reinforcement on the front line of the organization. With several levels of management, the senior leader must ensure that reinforcement reaches the front line of the organization. Therefore, leaders must positively reinforce their direct reports for the behavior of reinforcing. It is the leader's job to make sure that reinforcement is available to all who earn it and that it is delivered in an effective way.

Velocity

The most effective leaders are those who can mobilize the followers quickly. Adlai Stephenson, former Ambassador to the United Nations under President John F. Kennedy, once said, "When I give a speech, people will say, 'That was a good speech.' When Kennedy gives a speech people say, 'Let's march!'" Making changes quickly is becoming more and more critical in today's business environment. A national retailer determined that delays in getting merchandise from the loading docks to the front of the stores cost the company millions of dollars in sales each year. When nuclear power plants have a planned outage for maintenance, the time the plant is out of service can cost up to a million dollars a day and an outage may last 50 days or more. It is easy to see the importance of getting every employee excited about getting every job done efficiently.

You build a sense of urgency when you provide reinforcement for those who take action quickly. Modern organizations spend way too much time getting ready to respond. While planning and organizing should not be given short shrift, paralysis by analysis is more common than it is rare. Make sure that the followers who spring into action receive positive reinforcement and plenty of it.

If you have several layers of management, check with the followers to see how much time it takes to get action at the front-line level. If you make an announcement in the morning, go out into the office or plant, or call or e-mail remote performers toward the end of that day to see who knows about the change, if they know what to do, and if they have taken action. If you have this data, you will know where your problems are and what to do about them. Remember, the data should be used to positively reinforce those who respond accurately and correctly, not to punish those who don't. The followers who are not responding tell us more about our management process than it tells us about them. If everybody but one person responds to the call, you may have spotted an individual with a behavior that needs correcting. If a number of people don't respond, you are rarely looking at a performance problem—unless that performer is you! More than likely, a lack of timely response from a number of people is the result of some defect in your management system.

Since reinforcers can accelerate the rate of a behavior, frequency of reinforcement should be a concern of leaders when speed of response is an issue. Many leaders think that the magnitude of a reinforcer can make up for the frequency. More small reinforcers are more powerful than fewer large ones, even very large ones. Bonuses delivered annually have little motivational value. Leaders must be most concerned with how reinforcement is delivered every day—not at the end of the quarter or end of the year.

Direction

Speed of response has value only if one is speeding in the right direction. A joke told in many organizations these days is, "We're lost, but we're making good time." Because most employees have more things to do than they have time to do them, leaders must make sure that followers are focused on those things that are most important to the accomplishment of the result. This can be done in several ways. First, make sure you have identified the critical behaviors that produce a valuable result. What are the critical few? Answer the question, "What are 20% of the things that the followers do that produce 80% of the impact I need?" Once you know this, eliminate distractions and obstacles to doing them. This may mean that you have to take some work away from the followers so that they have more time to spend on your initiative, or that you change priorities and make other work less critical.

Having done these things, you must increase reinforcement for the critical behaviors that were identified earlier.

In his work on what is now called *The Matching Law* psychologist Richard Herrnstein (1997) demonstrated that behavior flows to the most reinforcing part of the environment. If you see that people are distracted from what you consider to be the most critical work, it tells you that the level of reinforcement for your priority work is minimal compared to reinforcement that is available for doing other things. You either have to remove reinforcement for the other behavior or increase reinforcement for the priority work.

Our instincts often lead us to react to a lack of momentum in ways that run counter to our intentions. Dr. Thomas Mawhinney (2005), professor of business psychology, has shown that leaders, as they experience less influence on follower behavior, tend to increase the frequency of punishment. He also has shown that the optimum performance conditions are reached when the follower and leader are reinforced for the same things and where reinforcement for non-mission essential choices are limited.

Generally speaking, it is more productive to increase the amount of time and attention you give to followers who are engaged in on-task behavior than to try to eliminate distractions. In the computer age, new distractions are being created faster than you can eliminate them. People can surf the Web, play games on their personal phones, take pictures, send pictures, talk to peers about all of these activities, or spend hours on work that is low on the priority list. You change direction by shifting reinforcers from one activity to another. How quickly the followers change what they are doing and how focused they are is a direct measure of how much reinforcement you have put on your priorities. Mass, velocity, and direction are determined by who gets reinforced, what gets reinforced, and how much reinforcement is delivered for on-task behavior.

chapter 16

BUILDING
COMMITMENT

Nothing in this world can take the place of persistence. Talent will not;
nothing is more common than unsuccessful people with talent.
Genius will not; unrewarded genius is almost a proverb. Education will not;
the world is full of educated derelicts.
Persistence and determination alone are omnipotent. The slogan "press on" has
solved and always will solve the problems of the human race.

Calvin Coolidge

Since leaders can neither be everywhere nor do everything, their success depends on their ability to build a significant level of commitment for their objectives among the followers. The employees' commitment must be such that they continue working toward those objectives in spite of the obstacles and distractions that are inevitable. And it must be such that progress in that direction produces a sense of satisfaction and well-being in the follower. If the only response to progress is simply relief, then every succeeding task becomes more difficult.

Commitment on anyone's part comes from the perception that they, and perhaps others, will be better off as a result of either acting in a particular way or by achieving certain goals. Commitment has the effect of producing both an obligation on the part of the person to act in certain ways and of producing satisfaction in the progress and achievement they experience. Effective leaders utilize both aspects of commitment—obligation and self-satisfaction—to build the level of commitment they need.

Many leaders, unwittingly, begin with a focus on obligation. They will use some threat, real or perceived, to galvanize the organization and push it to action. In their personal approach, they are stern and demanding with little tolerance for mistakes and failure. Their leadership methods are generously described as tough. In and of itself, this is not a problem, but when that leader does not produce in the followers a sense of satisfaction from their actions, that leader will fail a test of leadership. In that situation, the response of the followers is not likely to be that of discretionary effort. It is more likely to be that of the sergeant when confronted by his lieutenant with the statement: "Sergeant, I'll bet you hate me so much that when I die, you will probably come and spit on my grave." His answer was, "No sir, Lieutenant. I promised myself that when I get out of this man's army, I ain't gonna stand in line for nothing."

From a leadership perspective, we believe that the most important components of building commitment are creating a vision for the followers, defining the hierarchy of values that control decision making, and developing the persistence the followers show in staying the course until the commitment has been satisfied. While fundamentally simple, the devil is in the details.

Articulating the Vision

Ever since Peter Drucker's book, *Management: Tasks, Responsibilities, Practices,* was published in 1973, it has been a common management practice to write mission statements. This was later expanded to add vision and values statements as well. These were printed on handouts and posted on walls. Every decade has expanded these statements so that they are now usually quite lengthy documents. The simple act of expanding them illustrates the lack of utility. They have become propaganda in far too many organizations; yet, they are much too important for this fate.

A mission statement is a concise statement of why the organization or a job exists. It is defined by its customers, its products, and its services. It is a key tool for rationalizing the work of any organization and for clarifying the specific and essential contributions of the performers. Usually short, two to five words, a mission statement is initially enlightening to job holders who have never gone through the exercise. Once written, the reaction is typically, "Of course!" With familiarity, however, people begin to want more. The mission tells them *what* to do. What they next want to know is *why* they should do it.

The purpose of a vision statement is to provide the context people need to give value to the daily tasks they must complete. People did not enlist in the military services in World War II to fight the war. They didn't join to beat the enemy. They joined to free the world of a menace to their values of freedom and human dignity and to their way of life. Had there been a way to accomplish this without war, they would have gladly pursued that alternative instead.

The mission is always subordinate to the vision. The vision gives meaning to the mission. Where the mission gives the followers focus, the vision gives them energy. Under John Schueler, when he was President and Chief Operating Officer, the *Orange County Register* newspaper had a clear mission: sell newspapers. Their vision, however, was to become the primary source of information in Orange County, California, which meant that they had to take market share from the *Los Angeles Times*. This vision got everyone involved. Schueler made sure that everyone, from the carriers to the reporters, knew what they had to do to help make the vision a reality. Therefore, he provided them with concrete ways to measure progress which, in turn, set the occasion for celebrating their role in making it happen.

The Biblical verse, Proverbs 29:18, is often quoted in leadership literature. To paraphrase it, "Without a vision, the people perish." Why would the lack of a vision cause people to perish? The most common reason given is that a vision gives people hope. Why does lack of hope cause people to perish? Again, the most obvious answer is that without hope, there is nothing to live for. All productive and happy people have a vision of what success looks like. We have visions of getting our children through college and of our children becoming happy adults. We have visions of going on a vacation or buying a house. Working for the realization of these things causes people to endure hardship, work long hours, and forego immediate pleasures in order to reach long-term goals. How does this translate to business? Does your organization's vision give people something to work for? Does it give them a meaning for their hard work and sacrifice or does it give them hope that they can achieve some of their own dreams and aspirations?

At the time of this writing, two teams are preparing to meet in the Super Bowl. Players have been heard to say many times that playing in the Super Bowl was the vision they had when they began playing the sport. It is easy to see how a vision of playing in the Super Bowl in early February could motivate players six months earlier during summer practices. This is the venue where all professional players want to end the season. They know that not only will they receive money and publicity, but they will receive admiration from family, friends, fans, coaches, and management. Analogies can be found in most organized sports. Is it possible for an organization to create the same involvement, excitement, and enthusiasm about its success as sports teams do with their players and customers? The answer is, "Absolutely!"

While the mission statement is a management tool, the vision is a leadership tool. Once you determine the mission, the manager's focus is on execution. However, rather than keeping his head down and becoming preoccupied with the successful accomplishment of the mission, the leader must constantly scan the horizon to find those things that provide the next opportunity to grow the organization. The products, strategies, and other innovations that the leader chooses should have a high probability of success. Roger Milliken, president of Milliken & Company, was excellent at this. He anticipated the trend in the 1970s for double knit fabrics, went to Europe to find the best knitting machine on the market, and promptly bought two years' of company production of the machines. When double knits became the rage, he was the only one who could produce the best fabrics. When everybody else got into the market, he sold most of his machines and purchased flatbed knitting machines. He was willing to abandon present technology as quickly as something better appeared on the horizon. Because he had such a high success rate with the ways he moved the organization, employees were quick to follow when he wanted to change directions.

Sports have it easier than business because the mission and vision almost never change. The mission is to win games. The vision is to be the champions. Since all players know what to do and where they stand in realizing the vision, most of them have passion for their respective sports.

In organizations, the vision comes from the leader's ability to see in two directions. The first is to look beyond the borders of the organization and identify those factors which will define the enterprises' success in the future. Success factors may be in terms of the political, economic, or social environment, the changing demographics relative to age, income, and so on, or many other factors such as evolving technology. They all ask what the consumers of their products or services will demand in the future. Those who are best at predicting customer behavior are those who understand the laws of behavior and spend time researching the changing reinforcement patterns of their customers.

The second direction the leader looks is toward the followers. Here the leader identifies for the organization's performers the changes that are required to deliver these reinforcers to the customers. The key is to do this in such a way that each person can clearly see the benefits of the changes they will be asked to make. In sports, the vision is so well-understood that each player clearly knows what the consequences are personally and for the team. It is rarely clear how the organization's success will affect individuals, other than allowing them to keep their jobs. Employees are rarely passionate about the organization's vision when job retention is their only personal outcome.

One of our clients had an outstanding year, so much so that the company newsletter's headline read, "Banner Year!" Inside on the first page was a letter from the president telling everyone that the new year's goals would involve belt tightening and more demanding performance targets. We pointed out to him that this was an apparent contradiction. The average employee reading this would probably explain this as management's greed. The president explained that they knew their competitor was building a new factory which, from the moment it came online, would produce a competitive product cheaper and better than they could make. After some thought, they determined that their emphasis going forward would be to beat the competition at their own game as opposed to asking for more sacrifice and harder work. The vision of besting the competition was much more energizing and reinforcing to the employees and had the effect of generating higher performance and lower costs.

For a leader, the vision is a way of helping the followers become players in the game and not just cogs in the machine. The vision allows them to participate in some undertaking that is greater and more interesting than they would otherwise have. It generates the feeling of being a part of the in crowd—those who rub shoulders with successful people; and, it gives them the sense of having earned the right of access to this club by their contributions to the vision.

Values

The second source of satisfaction comes from knowing that you won the right way. Winning is not everything. Many distance runners take great pleasure in the sacrifice and dedication they commit to the sport, and sometimes become somewhat self-righteous in their attitude toward those who are not willing to invest as much as they do. They also begin to look down on cheating and cheaters. Winning is important, but winning on merit is truly rewarding.

Bobby Jones, the most celebrated amateur in the history of golf, called a penalty on himself because his ball moved as he addressed it. Even though no one saw it, he assessed himself a penalty, causing him to lose the tournament by one stroke. To him, his personal integrity and the integrity of the game were more important than winning.

In a similar manner through his research on learned industriousness, Robert Eisenberger (1992) shows that people who are reinforced for delivering discretionary effort are more industrious and more honest than people who do not have such a reinforcement history. The implication for the leader is that the environment should be structured in such a way that those employees who put in extra effort get recognized and rewarded as they are doing it. This is different from the manner most organizations reward employees who meet or exceed their goals. Results tell you little about the behavior involved in achieving them, and rewarding results may, or may not, reinforce the kinds of behaviors that benefit the organization.

Winning the right way is what values are all about. Which shortcuts are permissible and which are not? Which decisions conform to the values and which ones violate them? What is the difference between promoting a product and deceiving the customer? How should the performer interpret the leader's remarks, such as "I don't care how you do it. Just get it done"? In your organization, how do you make a decision about how much and what kind of information you share with employees, regulators, or shareholders? All of these ethical questions have an impact on both the organization and the performers within it. Values are our guide to answering the truly important questions in the absence of specific instructions.

Values have the property of either binding people to each other or of dividing them from one another. Common values define religious groupings, political factions, and activist groups of all kinds. They are also the battleground for these same factions. They define the lenses that people use to interpret data. The percentage of Americans living in poverty is either a matter of pride or a matter of shame, depending on the values of the observer. One side points to the fact that the United States has one of the lowest poverty rates in the world. The other points to the millions who fall below the poverty line.

In business, people do not openly talk about their values; yet they are always talking and acting in ways that demonstrate them. When values are not discussed, the observers interpret them in light of their own understanding. When the leader asks for sacrifice, some people comply and some people sneer. While it is not necessary that every single person comply for an organization to be successful, it is not reasonable to leave the interpretation of our values to each individual. Leaders must work diligently to ensure that there is a common understanding of how work will be done and how decisions will be reached.

The purpose of stating an organization's values, then, is to allow individuals clear self-management opportunities and to unite these individuals so that more of them form bonds of common interest with others and with the organization's objectives. The resulting reduction in conflict and increase in self-directed activity in pursuit of the vision permits the leader to focus more energy on the critical functions of his position.

So, leaders must state the values they believe to be key for the business and explain them. What's more, they can expect everyone else to do the same. But we know that stating your values is not enough. In "The Kindnesses of Children," an unpublished study by David Rosenhan (1969), the author concluded: "Moral preachings have no effect on behavior. If the model behaves charitably so will the child—even if the model has preached greed. And conversely, if the model preaches charity, but practices greed, the child will follow the model's precept and will not contribute to the charity. *Behavior in the prosocial area is influenced by behavior, not by words.*"

Bud Grant, the long-time coach of the Minnesota Vikings during their heyday, used to start training camp by showing rookies how the team stood at attention for the National Anthem. He had a respected veteran show, in detail, how to hold the helmet under his left arm with the mask facing forward, with his toes touching the sideline stripe. He did not leave it to chance that all the players knew how to show respect for the anthem and the flag, one of his values. Talking about values should not be thought of as silly, trivial, or old-fashioned. For this reason, a leader should choose values she willingly accepts and believes in rather than mimic the values of other organizations or choose those that look or sound good.

Values can take on a religious or philosophical overtone if you do not relate them to the activities the followers pursue every day. This involves providing relevant examples from the organization, taken either from actual and/or hypothetical situations that illustrate how the values were adhered to or how they were ignored. These examples and non-examples should range from the black-and-white to those with light shades of gray. Generalizing from others' experiences to our own situation requires us to make many fine discriminations before we can internalize them or make them habitual.

One of the primary reasons leaders should publicly recognize individuals for ethical choices is to provide meaningful examples to others. We do not always learn from others' failures. If we did, we would have significantly fewer criminals in our society and thus fewer criminal acts. On the other hand, one of the more powerful influences on behavior in the workplace is an example of a peer or leader. When the leader can identify many individuals as models for ethical conduct, the leader's burden to always be on display is lessened.

Getting individuals to openly discuss their decisions in light of the ethics concerned provides them with an opportunity for reinforcement. We learn best from the consequences of our own behavior. This can be difficult for the individual and tricky for leadership. If someone confesses to an ethical lapse, how do you respond? For the individual, confessing involves taking a risk with the leader's response. An organization we know had a stated value of personal integrity that involved a policy of self-reporting errors. It also had a policy that certain types of errors or omissions could result in job termination. The leadership never saw the conflict, but the employees certainly did. Some people in the organization claimed that self-reporting was a consistent practice, while other people snickered at this belief.

Leaders must be consistent in making decisions based on values. Inconsistent application of values leads to the abandonment of the value. This means that consideration of values important to the organization should be done deliberately and seriously as they place an obligation on leadership that cannot be delegated. Enron is probably the most blatant example. In the book, *The Smartest Guys in the Room* authors McLean and Elkind (2003) detail numerous and obvious violations of the company's stated values. If this state of affairs had been attended to by Enron leadership, Enron's history would have been very different today. When employees were told to be aggressive in the marketplace, there were almost no limits on the behavior that was rewarded as long as that behavior resulted in increased revenue and cash flow. Every time a deal was completed and condoned that was somewhat questionable as to its legality or morality, the acceptance of the deal led to more questionable future deals. Transgressions, even those considered minor, cannot be ignored.

For leadership, all policies and decisions should be evaluated from a values perspective. How do you make your decisions? Do they stand up to scrutiny under the light of your stated values? Even ethical people make decisions that are not consistent with the values they profess. How many times have we heard of some religious leader caught in an immoral act? How often have we watched business leaders on trial for ethical lapses? How often have we seen presidential nominees withdraw after scrutiny of their personal lives? For many of these people, their failure was a lapse, not a pattern of corruption. Permitting your decisions to be examined for their ethical implications is simply a practical precaution and a significant signal to the organization about the worth and contribution of ethical behavior.

Persistence

One of the hallmarks of commitment is the persistence of the followers in pursuit of the goal. How do they deal with setbacks and failure? Are they resilient or do they break under the weight of adversity? Are they distracted by other opportunities that are peripheral to the cause? Much as a drummer sets the pace for the band, the leader sets the pace for the organization. Whether you recognize it or not, goals set by the leader establish the minimum performance standard, not the optimum. Unlike the band leader, the leader in business or industry hopes performance will exceed this minimum pace.

Perhaps the model of persistence that we want in business is that of the marathon runner. They run long distances, in all kinds of weather, without regard to minor aches and pains, and most of them can only expect a tee shirt (which they pay for) and the self-satisfaction that comes from finishing the race. Great leaders produce the same characteristics in their followers. But most of them have to train this persistence in order to get it, since natural consequences typically work against it.

Much as the marathoner begins by running laps or short distances, the leader trains his followers in small steps. If you don't get positive reinforcement for small steps, you probably won't stay with it. The equivalent to running laps in business is meeting commitments. It is so fundamental to accomplishment that it is easy to overlook the training opportunity. Leaders are insistent on meeting commitments they make to their followers as well as insisting that followers meet commitments made to the leader. If it does not work both ways, it does not work long.

Training for persistence is relatively easy. All that is required is that someone records the commitments that are made and then gives the individual credit as the commitments are met. One senior level executive made it a practice to record all commitments that were made during his staff meetings. Commitments were written on a flip chart and the next meeting began with a review of the commitments and progress against the list. When a commitment was met, he acknowledged the success. When the commitment was not met, the reasons were briefly discussed and the commitment was re-tasked. The most common reason for failure was overly ambitious goal setting by the followers. Can this be said of most followers? Unfortunately, most leaders instinctively react negatively to any failure and thereby lose this form of discretionary effort. The followers then begin to sandbag and confine themselves to making commitments they are certain of meeting. This form of playing it safe has a huge cost. In this organization, over time, more and more commitments were met as the leader observed that encouraging the smaller commitments that were met was more motivational than setting fewer and larger ones where the probability of success was lower.

When you set commitments small enough, you have many more training opportunities. One of the most common problems with project milestones is that they are too large. Consequences for meeting or missing these due dates come so seldom that all they do is train people to procrastinate. And, as we all know, "haste makes waste," so those last minute rushes to meet deadlines work against efficiency and effectiveness in the organization.

When people are trained properly to meet their commitments, they develop a sense of obligation to the leader. They strive harder to avoid disappointing him. In such organizations, the leader rarely has to raise his voice, express anger, or show other emotional responses to follower failure. The follower often punishes himself much more severely than the leader ever would. For this kind of leader, the frequency of disappointment is low.

Like the marathoner who gains endurance by slowly adding distance to his practices, followers build persistence when the leader reinforces follower effort toward some long-term goal. Of course, it should go without saying that the marathoner celebrates completion of the race. Leaders need to define small successes and take time to celebrate when they occur.

chapter 17

INCREASING

INITIATIVE

*The highest and best form of efficiency is
the spontaneous cooperation of a free people.*

Bernard Baruch (1921)

Teamwork

Wouldn't it be great to work in a place where everyone likes each other and where everyone is focused on improving the enterprise every day? Most managers think this occurs only in dreams. Granted, organizations like this are rare, but they do exist. Although personal relationships are a private matter, having a team that works together is a leader's responsibility. However, having an organization where people work well together is not the leader's primary goal. The primary goal is to get people to work together for the betterment of the enterprise.

Many things that leaders do can result in destructive competition between team members, blaming co-workers, and even lying. Policies, incentives, and appraisal systems are just a few of a leader's responsibilities that can have an impact on how peers relate to each other. The right policies, incentives, rewards, and recognition can facilitate teamwork. These same systems, when poorly designed and executed, can cause team members to work at cross purposes. Frequent negative behavior on the part of peers toward each other is, in the final analysis, a reflection of poor leadership.

Just because you have teams does not mean that you have teamwork. It is our experience that teams are, by and large, poorly managed. Most managers readily accept the 80/20 rule as it applies to teams— 20% of the team members produce 80% of the results. Unfortunately, many managers accept that as human nature because they see this same pattern of effort in their churches, civic clubs, and in volunteer groups in which very few people do most of the work. Of course, this is not human nature but a reflection of the way consequences are managed within the team or group.

Leaders certainly haven't received much help from team literature. Most of the literature on work teams is either experiential or common sense rather than scientific and, as such, is subject to much error. For example, most books on teams suggest that team members should be rewarded equally. While common sense would tell you that this is true, behavioral science tells us that it is not. When there is unequal effort in team accomplishment, there should be unequal distribution of reinforcement. What do you think handing out equal rewards does to the 20% who produced 80% of the results? It is not a good idea to punish your best performers. It is the leader's job to ensure equal effort. When equal effort doesn't exist, positive and negative consequences should be used to correct the problem.

As a leader, you may not know the details of which team members contributed to an accomplishment and which members did not. Therefore, before you go public with the accomplishment, find out about the individual efforts of the members. Then, when you announce the results, the team members who did most of the work will know that you know. One of the problems that leaders have, particularly if they are removed from the followers, is that the high performing individuals don't know if bosses know about their extra effort. Knowing that the boss knows is reinforcing to most people in the workplace today. In a team-oriented workplace when the numbers are compiled for upper management review, it is impossible to see individual effort. In many cases, learning and acknowledging the 20% who produced 80% of the work is sufficient to keep them motivated for a period of time.

You cannot positively reinforce a team, only the behavior of team members. As a leader, you must make sure that someone knows the reinforcers of each team member and that, whenever possible, those reinforcers are used to reinforce individual effort. It is always appropriate to reinforce teamwork behavior. Resist the temptation to make gratuitous remarks about how everyone did their part and pulled together. Unless you know this for a fact, these comments can destroy your credibility and create ill feelings among the team members. To avoid these errors, a leader needs to be proactive in maintaining contact with members as they make progress toward the accomplishment. Don't wait until the team reaches the final goal to meet with team members. Regular interactions will mean not only that you know more about what is going on, but your contact will indicate your interest and the importance of what the team members are doing. This alone will provide reinforcement for the ongoing effort.

Teamwork is really about managing relationships. It is clear to any leader that the followers must cooperate with each other for the best result and be proactive in assisting others when the need or opportunity arises. Leaders want a team in which members don't wait to be asked to help, but remain constantly in touch with what is going on with other members so that they know how to help one another. People who have been reinforced for helping others get a lot of personal satisfaction when they know that what they have done is helpful and appreciated. When teams don't have these relationships, it falls to the leader to correct it.

Bud Clay, former vice president of research for AG Communications in Phoenix, Arizona, noted that his managers were so overloaded with their own problems that they felt they had no disposable time to help their team members. From his perspective, he knew that two managers working in adjacent offices may each know something that would help the other solve a priority problem. He also knew that the person helping their peer solve a problem would receive help with one of his own priorities. Sue Webber, Bud's performance manager, came up with an idea which seemed pretty bizarre at first, but worked amazingly well. She put a large glass jar in the middle of the conference room table and labeled it the "Dead Monkey Jar." This theme played off of the common expression of "having a monkey on my back." Each time a manager helped a colleague get a monkey off his back, the manager on the receiving end would write a thank you note to his colleague, record it in the log book kept in the conference room, and then place a small plastic monkey in the Dead Monkey Jar. Teamwork was measured by the number of inches of monkeys in the jar. As Sue was somewhat concerned that some of the managers would think this was silly, she gave them an opportunity to stop using the Dead Monkey Jar after a couple of months. They chose to keep the jar and continued using it for several more months with impressive results.

A device we have used for years with our customers with uniformly positive results is an "I was helped by . . . " chart. In any work setting where it is essential for people to work together for the benefit of the organization and the customer, we hung a chart on the wall listing all employees. Then we would give each person a sticker that identified who that person was. When one helped another, the one who was helped would put her sticker by that person's name on the chart. You could soon see at a glance who was helping whom. The change a simple chart makes in the culture is amazing. Not only does it give recognition for those who help, but it is an antecedent for the others to take the initiative in finding ways they can help other team members. By the way, we have never introduced this in a workplace where the people considered this to be silly. We think this is true because it made visible the teamwork behavior that was heretofore invisible to those inside and outside the unit.

Managing Interfaces

When leaders have more followers than they can personally manage, the leadership task becomes that of managing the interfaces, or relationships, of the units in an organization. Conflict between units is so common that many leaders think that it is inevitable and, believe it or not, there are some leaders who encourage conflict. We know of a company where the president encouraged fighting between his management team. He stated that unless they were willing to fight for something, it was probably not important. His team hated not only him but each other as well. This president could get away with such antics for awhile because the company was the industry leader. He did not see the long-term impact of his behavior on his managers and on company performance; the company ultimately lost its marketplace leadership.

Classic battles are waged between sales and manufacturing where goals are often incompatible. Manufacturing is rewarded by how cheaply it can manufacture a product, while sales is rewarded on dollars produced. Manufacturing wants one model in one size and one color. Sales, of course, wants ten models in many sizes and colors. The word *silo* is used so much in business that few people today know of its agricultural root. When conflicts arise between an organization's units, they are not inherent but are created by how consequences are arranged for the departments involved.

Goldratt (1999) wrote about the problem in his book, *Theory of Constraints.* He points out that cost accounting has ruined many companies since it causes the various units of the organization to minimize costs in certain parts of the process without considering what that practice does to the receiving unit. His basic message is that an organization's output is defined by the amount produced by the bottleneck, and that clearing the bottleneck becomes a priority for management.

Let's say that we have a company with three departments—Department A, Department B, and Department C. Each department produces 100 parts per hour, each part to be assembled into the final product. In a balanced production line, output for the final product would be 100 units per hour.

Balanced Production Line

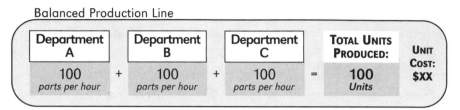

Let's also say that the manager of Department B decides that if he can produce 10 more parts per hour his cost per part will go down. In the typical organization, Department B manager receives some positive attention—public recognition, a bonus, or a very favorable performance review. But let's look at what happened to the company.

Unbalanced Production Line

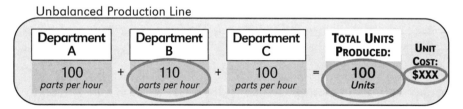

The production is still 100 units per hour, but the cost has actually gone up! We have more goods in process, consuming raw material and resources, and we have product that must be stored while waiting to be processed by Department C. In the well-run organization, we would want employees to help clear the bottleneck or to make improvements that would not impact negatively on the other departments. In the case mentioned, a cost improvement in Department B is a cost improvement only if it reduces the cost of manufacturing the finished product. The leadership trick is to get the followers to be as concerned with the final cost as they are with reducing cost in their part of the process.

How do you create an organization where managers don't build silos and where people in one part of the company will forsake a short-term accomplishment in their own unit to help another unit with its accomplishment? Managing interfaces is about managing reinforcement. The ability of a leader to pull reinforcers from one behavior and put it on another is at the heart of an agile, efficient, and customer-focused organization. The methodology for doing this is explained by Herrnstein's Matching Law. This law provides leaders with the methodology for changing behavior in individuals or organizations in an efficient and effective way. The Matching Law, also known as Herrnstein's Hyperbola,

Herrnstein's Hyperbola

$$B = k\left(\frac{r}{r+r_e}\right)$$

B = the rate of a behavior or the probability that it will occur

k = the asymptote, or the highest known performer

r = the number of reinforcers received for B

r_e = the number of reinforcers received for non-B

states, in effect, that the behavior is determined by the amount of reinforcement available for it, as well as the amount of reinforcement received for all other behaviors. In other words, behavior will flow to the most reinforcing part of the environment. When the implications of the Matching Law are fully understood, it is easy to understand what causes people to concentrate or focus on the job at hand. High rates of reinforcement are associated with focus; low rates are associated with high distractibility. Many managers think that concentration is a willful act, but concentration is a function of the concentration of reinforcement. People can concentrate when there is more reinforcement for a given task than is available in other parts of their environment. Therefore, it is more effective to increase reinforcement for the important tasks than to admonish someone to concentrate or stay focused.

Someone involved in routine work who receives little attention or reinforcement will be easily distracted and may relish the opportunity to help someone else. Those who are highly reinforced for the tasks at hand may be resistant to helping others. This is often observed when employees who are paid on the basis of their production resent anything that will pull them off of their work. While this is a good thing, it does not help when the organization is faced with problems outside those departments or units. In that case, it is important for the leader to shift reinforcers from one set of behaviors to another. In the case of the bottleneck above, the leader must make clearing the bottleneck a highly reinforcing event.

Careful examination of the Matching Law reveals that there are two ways to elicit an increase in behavior. One is the obvious: reinforce more. The second involves eliminating or reducing reinforcement for competing or distracting behaviors. Make sure that followers get reinforcement only for behaviors that are mission critical. Today, the workplace is increasingly filled with distractions that pull employees away from work, ranging from discussing politics, spreading company rumors and gossip, to e-mailing friends and surfing the Web. All these things take time away from behavior that advances the organization. As the number of distractions increase, it is impossible to monitor and limit them all. Therefore, the only way to maintain control is to increase the reinforcement available for desired behaviors.

Every year billions of dollars are wasted by companies in mergers and acquisitions because leaders do not plan reinforcers for the new organization from day one of its existence. Leaders typically talk about what we call *blue sky;* that is, how everything is going to be in the great by and by. In the meantime, one can derive more reinforcement from listening to the latest rumor of terminations or inappropriate promotions than for doing things to move the new company ahead. Rather than promise some future benefit, leaders must concentrate their efforts on how to make the followers' first contact with the new company a positive one. When leaders do this, little momentum is lost and the publicly stated reasons for the merger or acquisition are much more likely to be realized. The natural reinforcers in any change are likely to be for non-productive behaviors; therefore, leaders must increase reinforcement for productive behaviors.

Creativity *Is* Behavior

Although innovation and creativity will not give a company competitive advantage, it does keep a company in the marketplace. Innovation and creativity are necessary, but not sufficient, for organizations to thrive. For survival and/or success, companies must innovate at a rate superior to their competitors. To do this, leaders must develop an environment that supports creative behavior. Unfortunately, most innovation in this country occurs by accident—more than 98% according to Robinson and Stern (1997). This tells us that most corporate creativity is a by-product of other activities. While we are certainly glad that employees capitalize on accidental discoveries, the organization certainly cannot bet its future on serendipity. Leaders need a more predictable way to manage the process of innovation. Although we will not rehash the Japanese story here, it is clear that they manage innovation in a way superior to the United States. A company we visited in Japan had a suggestion rate per employee 981 times the average U.S. rate. Based on population, Japan produces three times as many patents as the United States. Clearly, they are doing something different in managing this process. A saying quoted by our Japanese host, that "many raindrops make an ocean" aptly describes their innovative process. They don't wait for the big breakthrough; they celebrate every improvement no matter how small.

Innovation and creativity are easier to lead than most people think. When you understand that creativity is about behavior, it is infinitely more manageable than if you think that creativity is a brain thing. Creativity comes from people doing new things or doing old things differently. The principles described in this book are as applicable to creativity and innovation as they are to the most repetitive task you can imagine, but you must first divest yourself of the notion that some people are more creative than others. All behavior is creative; some are more valued than others. People never do the same thing twice in exactly the same way. Managers are aware of this because they are constantly trying to eliminate variance from established processes. Leaders, on the other hand, are constantly trying to introduce variance as a means of coming up with something that is more attractive to their customers, whether it is lower cost, higher quality, or more functionality.

When you understand that creativity is behavior, you are well on the way to increasing it. Since you know that behavior that is reinforced will occur more often, one way to increase creativity is to positively reinforce variation. It is rather amazing that leaders tell followers that they want their ideas, but when they get the ideas either punish or fail to reinforce the employees who offered them. For many followers, suggesting an improvement is a novel behavior. However, telling someone that they have a great idea and then asking them to write it up can be enough to dissuade that person from making another suggestion. Even worse is when someone does write a suggestion, but then never knows if anyone ever took the trouble to read it. The leader must make it easy to talk about ideas and get them into some evaluation process. Have someone help the person write up their suggestion or ask them to describe their idea in detail to someone who will write it up and help them develop it.

Never have a "best idea of the year" award or anything resembling competition in this area. Also, don't pay for ideas. Instead, pay for the successful implementation of the ideas and pay all those who helped make them work. This is an arena in which some version of gainsharing is valuable. If the contingencies of reinforcement are correct, everyone will try to make every good idea work. We have seen many organizations where those who are responsible for evaluating and implementing ideas are punished—not intentionally, but by the processes used in the business. Engineers often have the task of evaluating suggestions as a minor part of their job and as such see it as an imposition, not as a source of personal reinforcement. People on the line see experimenting with a new process as interfering with the way they are paid or evaluated. Stopping what they are doing to set up some trial, run it, and then tear it down and reset normal operations again brings nothing but negatives for the average employee. The leader must set the policies, systems, and processes in such a way that everyone—*everyone*—is excited about improvement. Remember, it is the leader's job to value improvement. The smaller the improvement one can see and reinforce, the faster the change.

The second way to increase creativity is to put the old way of doing things on extinction. Joel Barker (1993) wrote a book called *Paradigms: The Business of Discovering the Future* in which he tells managers to "bust your paradigms." It is very difficult to will yourself to "think outside the box." As Tuli Kupferberg, the poet, said, "When patterns are broken, new worlds emerge." The problem is that leaders usually see a need *before* patterns are broken. The followers may be doing just fine. They have a routine with which they are comfortable and productive. The leader may know that incremental improvement on an existing method or product will not meet the future needs of the business. In these cases, the leader may have to break a pattern in order to get creativity. He may have to say, "As of May 1st, I will no longer accept things done the old way." But he must be prepared for what will follow.

People in such a situation will usually try to innovate by making improvements on the old way. The leader must not accept these small improvements. Although usually valued, they are not of value in this instance. The next response from the employees may be to complain that the old way is now working better and that the required time frame is unreasonable. They may even question the sanity of the leader. These are all normal responses to the loss of reinforcement. These behaviors tell you that the creative process is working. Most leaders will give in to the complaining just about the time a creative breakthrough is imminent.

To use such an approach, you must have a workplace where positive reinforcement is the usual way of getting things done. If it is not, people will give up on the project or even quit because of the stress. By the way, the antidote for stress is—you guessed it—positive reinforcement. Before setting up the organization for breakthroughs, a leader must also know that a breakthrough is possible.

Breakthroughs will occur naturally in an environment that values improvement. Think of a workplace from which everyone left at the end of the day thinking about how they could do their job better tomorrow or about something that would improve the enterprise in some way. If followers are trying to make improvements every day, they will eventually reach the limits of equipment or current processes. In that instance, extinction will occur until a new way to work has been found.

Leaders must prepare the environment for creativity. They need to use antecedents and consequences toward that end. One of our customers who built high-end office furniture took the designers to modern art museums as a way of expanding their experience. 3M has traditionally done more than most organizations to facilitate creativity. They give employees time, money, and space to pursue even some of the most far-out ideas. For example, a pig farmer once called an employee in 3M's Adhesives Division to find out where he could get some automotive tape that 3M had discontinued. The employee asked why a pig farmer would want tape used for painting automobiles. The farmer explained that piglets, raised on concrete, fall and scrape their knuckles which often led to infection. The tape was flexible and the best thing he had found to tape the knuckles to prevent the scraping. The employee wondered if 3M could make pig socks. He was given the necessary resources to invent the product, which he did. Even though the product worked well, it did not appear to meet the return on investment 3M required on new products, so it never got to market. 3M has thousands of inventions like that. What they know is that while 100 of those inventions may never make it to market, one that is successful will more than pay for the thousands that didn't. Think Post-It Notes. Remember Thomas Edison's approach to invention? He did not treat ideas that didn't work as failures because they brought him at least one step closer to a solution.

A workplace in which people feel free to make suggestions about how to improve the operation is a mark of leadership. To foster such an environment, the leader must make sure that all improvements are valued; that is, all improvements are positively reinforced. Be prepared to reinforce ideas that are off the wall with the understanding that reinforcement of the behavior of thinking about how to be more effective is always reinforceable, even if the initial ideas are far removed from your final target. Make it easy for ideas to be heard. Just listening to an idea is a fruitful way to spend time, even precious leadership time. While leaders don't always need to involve themselves in developing and testing hypotheses about running the business better, they must make it easy and positive for others to do so. To capitalize on innovation and creativity, the leader must make sure that the implementation of an idea benefits everyone involved in its implementation. Make sure that policies, processes, and rewards favor the successful implementation of an idea. Ideas have value only when they lead to a positive outcome for the organization. Think what would happen to your organization if every employee presented an idea for improving the enterprise at least once a week for a year. It is possible. Think about the momentum, commitment, and teamwork that this activity would create!

chapter 18

RECIPROCITY: MAXIMIZING LEADER & FOLLOWER INTERACTIONS

The mutual confidence on which all else depends can be maintained only by an open mind and a brave reliance upon free discussion.

Learned Hand (1952)

. . . their dependence mutual and their obligations reciprocal.

Lucretia Mott (1849)

Leaders often share warm, personal relationships with followers. For many, these personal relationships extend beyond the time spent working together. Some of these relationships even extend into retirement. But just as likely is the possibility that leaders have relationships with their employees that never extend beyond the professional level. Many people focus so tightly on the work that they have little to offer others in the way of personal interactions.

For leaders, this lack of time for personal interaction will always be a disadvantage in the pursuit of their goals. All men and women are social creatures who require personal contacts with others to function effectively. When they cannot find meaningful relationships in one person or one group, they seek it in other places. People focus on the relationships that provide meaning to their efforts. Most employee failure is not so much a failure of the individual as a person as it is a failure of the individual to find the necessary support and training from relationships at work.

We once worked at an automobile assembly plant that had recalled some of its retired managers to assist with a plant reconfiguration for new automobile models. In a meeting of all management and supervision, one retiree who had previously been the head of the maintenance department related his story. He had risen from an hourly laborer to the manager of hundreds of employees. Looking back over his years on the job, he said that he could remember 20 or so really "sorry workers." He could also remember 20-30 really outstanding performers. But, he said, "What keeps me up at night now is that most of the people who helped me go from supervisor to head of maintenance, I can't remember their names. I hope you won't make my mistake!"

Competence at work is a commodity. Ample evidence indicates that expert performance is the result of deliberate practice, not attitude or aptitude (Ericsson et al, 1993). In turn, this deliberate practice is something that a leader can teach someone else. The research on learned industriousness connects rewards, high effort, and persistence, which are also the basic components of deliberate practice (Eisenberger, 1989). Those who are not leaders never understand this. They think that finding competent management and followers is problematic and, for the poor leader, their personal history supports this conclusion. These leaders are hindered in bringing out the best in their people because they do not understand that they can only bring out the best in others through a personal effort of their own. People cannot perform at their best in an environment of pressure, fear of failure, and possible monetary rewards as the sole motive forces.

Many leaders play with fire when they keep followers who are self-centered. Some people will only follow if it promotes their immediate purposes. Without a personal relationship with the leader, people tend to use their position to further their own cause rather than the cause of the leader. Leaders need followers who will merge some of their own interests with the interests of the cause.

Several highly visible indicators reveal how effectively a leader builds relationships with his or her followers. Once again, these indicators are to be found in the behavior of the follower.

Respect

Respect, and its twin *deference,* is usually extended to the leader in organizations by the followers—at least initially. For leaders, maintaining that initial respect is the real measure of leadership skills, because respect is so easily lost. Once respect is lost, the leader must use the exercise of crude authority to promote his agenda. Much as the judge uses contempt citations to silence critics, a silenced dissident does not mean that respect exists. It simply means that the criticism is being delivered to another audience.

By the very nature of the decisions a leader must make to introduce change, respect is always in jeopardy. Many followers have their own ideas about which changes, if any, are needed and from their own vantage point, they develop genuine concerns about the implementation of a leader's new agenda. When change takes a long time, and when there is a history of mistrust between a follower and a leader, the pace of progress and the inevitable problems associated with introducing change all work to erode respect for the plan and for the planner.

One of the most respected characteristics of leaders is decisiveness. Of course this implies that most of the decisions prove to be effective. Making effective decisions depends on the leader having access to accurate and timely data. But rarely does data alone tell the leader enough. What really matters is the essence of the numbers, or how they were produced, and the meaning they have for the organization and the performers who created them. Ken Lay, of Enron fame, is still claiming that he didn't understand how the financial numbers of his company were being produced. He had the data but apparently failed to understand its significance as it related to the people and their behavior.

By the same token, we hear about market leaders who see trends before they develop. This comes from looking at data on consumer behavior and investigating the reasons for the consumers' choices. John Schueler, now President of the *Los Angeles Daily News*, calls this *drilling down*. The term implies that one goes to the source of the numbers—the people who create them—to understand the numbers' meaning. Once the relationships are understood, these leaders make effective decisions on how to best capitalize on consumer choices and how to make the best, ethical decisions.

In the same way, leaders make themselves accessible to their followers so that they can better understand the followers' choices. This requires leaders to establish a relationship with their followers such that the follower is willing to provide accurate, uncensored input. Beyond that, it requires that the followers are willing to seek out the leader to volunteer information rather than wait until they are asked. The followers must know the leader and his priorities and concerns well enough to know when information they have would be of interest to him.

Good leaders build relationships such that the followers are willing to confide in them. Issues of hierarchy and status are minimized in order to profit from a free flow of information that is useful to the organization's success. One of the best indicators of how well a leader is doing in this area is by looking at the number of employees or followers who confide personal information or who ask for advice or input on personal matters. If you do not know personal information about your followers, you cannot be certain that you understand them well enough to interpret their actions or communications.

All of this implies that leaders establish relationships of mutual respect with the followers. If the leader cannot show respect for the lowest member of the organization, many people will withhold respect for the leader. The negative impact this has on organizational performance is significant. Eisenberger (1989) outlines how our society creates laziness in a large portion of our society by not showing respect for menial work. The snobbery that suggests that the work of some individuals or groups is not as valuable as other contributions will always erode leadership impact. ADI's experience in unionized organizations shows us that this outlook is actually pretty pervasive in American industry and contributes in a significant way to adversarial relationships with management. When we place a high value on wealth and status, we may actually deny the value of work that is less well-remunerated or of lower status in the hierarchy. The damage this does to the free flow of ideas, suggestions, and information is incalculable.

Trust

People have difficulty following anyone they do not trust. Stated in positive terms, people tend to act on information they receive from people they trust when that information is useful to them. So, one of the first considerations of a leader is establishing a relationship of trust with the followers.

The test of trust comes when someone shows that they are willing to share information which might be harmful to themselves. It is easy to see its opposite. Mistakes and faults are hidden, or only reluctantly admitted in too many organizations. If followers trust their leader, mistakes and problems are discussed and corrective actions taken quickly, effectively, and relatively painlessly. The upside of trust in the leader is so significant to the organization that fostering that trust must be an ongoing concern.

The primary benefit of trust, from the leader's point of view, is that it accelerates learning. It is impossible to attribute cause correctly when you don't have critical information. Without an accurate identification of the cause of an event, it is nearly impossible to construct a cure. This is why so many management groups continually confront the same issues over and over. Our experience shows us that very few organizations ever really deal with the causes of simple issues such as perpetual absenteeism, high turnover, or frequent accidents even though those events bring very high costs. When individuals feel they must protect themselves from others, the cost of performance always increases.

Developing trust is conceptually easy, although the practice can be difficult. In essence, we trust people who do what they say they will do. So, to build trust, we must take more care in the commitments we make and even greater care in following those commitments through to completion. Failure to follow through will always result in a loss of trust. In almost all of the organizations where we find trust to be an issue, the root cause of the problem typically resides in a casual approach to making commitments that are later forgotten by those who made them. Leaders of such organizations show little discipline in recording or systematically tracking commitments to completion. Rarely do we find a problem in keeping commitments to be due to lack of integrity, although that is how not keeping one's commitments is ultimately interpreted by those who do not trust management.

Followers also learn to trust, or not to trust, the leader by looking at how the leader deals with mistakes and differing opinions. For this reason, leaders teach their followers to voice their opinions and to admit mistakes rather than holding their silence or hiding their errors. This can only be done if the leader is accessible. If people do not feel comfortable bringing their ideas to their leader while the ideas are still in the formative stage, fewer ideas at any stage will be forthcoming. Once the leader trains people to speak their minds freely or to confess to mistakes when they are made, the flow of information up the chain of command always expands dramatically. With this increased communication flow, the leader will always receive more useful information that functions as early warning signals or precursors to events that are significant to the leader and to the company. As a result, a leader who creates this environment of trust experiences fewer surprises.

One interesting example of how this kind of environment can be developed was offered by Vice Admiral George Dyer (1963). He relates the story of a rear admiral, new to his command of a destroyer flotilla, who circulated a new policy on Leave and Liberty, prior to his first staff meeting. At the meeting, he polled each of his staff officers for their comments regarding the new policy. One by one, they voiced their support with reservations. The flag secretary, the last person to be asked, replied, "It smells to high heaven." When asked about his statement, the flag secretary gave several specific reasons why the new policy was not a good one.

After the meeting, the admiral called the flag secretary into his office and confessed that he had written the policy so that it *would* stink in order to quickly learn who would give him honest advice and opinions. "I won't always agree with you in the future, but continue to give me your honest and frank opinions. I will appreciate them. You will profit by giving them to me."

Good leaders avoid micromanaging. This is a tough balancing act because some leaders know more about the details of the operations than any of their subordinates. Micromanagement does not come from what you know, but from *what you do with what you know.* Leaders use this knowledge to teach their followers what is important. Micromanagers use this knowledge to catch employee errors. Micromanagement is more of an ego game than a leadership practice. It is relatively easy for anyone to find a gap in even an expert's knowledge. Leaders who play this game tend to be competitive with their followers rather than supportive of them. The accusation of micromanagement is always an indictment of the leader and says in effect that the follower does not trust how the leader will deal with the information he gains from observing their work.

Leaders profit from their followers' willingness to express their opinions and points of view in order to learn more about the follower.

This is the best way to know what is or is not important to them. The knowledge of what is important to someone, in turn, shows you more precisely how to reinforce and motivate them. People work for what is important to them, not for what is important to others. Once you grasp this principle, gaining followers is much easier.

Grow Talent

Billy Beane, the general manager of the Oakland Athletics baseball team, has found a way to reduce his payroll by finding good players whom other clubs are not interested in pursuing. Beane has discovered behaviors that predict success in baseball, which differ from those traditionally used by baseball scouts (Lewis, 2003). As a result, Oakland has the lowest cost per win of any team in baseball. The problem is that, because of his success, other teams are now copying his methods, creating a bidding war for what were once low-cost players. As other teams sign these players, Beane's competitive edge is reduced as there are a limited number of these players available. Nordstrom's department store has a similar approach to hiring successful associates. They have discovered those traits that make for success in selling and hire only those people who meet those rather selective criteria.

The continued success of both Nordstrom's and the Oakland Athletics assumes an unlimited pool of applicants from which to choose. Population and educational statistics tell us that this is not the case. Every indication points to the fact that in the next 15 years, there will be a shortage of qualified people for many available jobs. If your organization is not good at growing talent, you may have jobs that go begging at the front line of the organization. Shortages at that level portend a shortage at leadership levels as well. Given the current failure rates of leaders, it should be clear that organizations must do things to create leaders within the ranks of the organization.

One of the primary responsibilities of a leader is to create leaders. This flies in the face of what Michaels, Handfield-Jones, Axelrod, et. al.

(2001) have led executives to believe in their book, *War for Talent.* They say that success in the future belongs to those organizations that recruit and retain top talent. We believe that there is no shortage of those already in your organization who can become leaders if your organization has effective leadership. Good talent is more of a commodity than most people believe.

Our definition of *talent* is "unrecognized practice." When you approach talent in this way, you can see immediately how to grow talent—increase opportunities for practice. Ericsson (1993) has discovered that expertise in any field is acquired by deliberate practice. It is not about native ability, as more than 96% of expertise in any field is attributed to practice alone. The key to developing people is to pinpoint the behaviors that are critical to any job function and provide guided practice of those behaviors. Of course, if talent is already available, you may want to forego the time and effort it takes to produce the talent on your own. You must realize that you are making that choice. It is not that present employees can't learn what is necessary but that you have decided that it is not worth the expenditure of the organization's resources to teach them.

As you approach the challenge of growing talent, it is helpful to understand that you don't teach someone to the *limit of their* ability; you teach them to the *limit of your* ability. We have no tests that can accurately predict another's capability. If you think employees can't do something, they will rarely disappoint you. If you think they can and you provide positive reinforcement for the effort, they will constantly surprise you by their achievements. Unless a company is in a growth mode, most companies have all the talent they need.

Followers develop their potential more fully when working with true leaders. This is because they have more examples of good leadership, of what success looks like, and they have more opportunities to learn the cost and the rewards of success through personal experience. You can tell the better leaders by the number of followers who are judged to be successful. In a similar vein, you can tell who is a poor leader by looking at the low success rates of his employees.

Positive Accountability Forum

One of the ways to provide managers with practice in using the concepts in *Measure of A Leader* is to hold a meeting in which those involved in helping the enterprise fulfill its mission have an opportunity to show the results (data) they have achieved. The format is usually to give each presenter three minutes to display a PowerPoint or overhead transparency of the objectives or projects they are working on and to talk about their results and the critical behaviors they are managing. Then allow questions from the attendees, but be sure to focus them on the details of what was done and how it was done, not on critical evaluation. The purpose of the meeting is to provide positive reinforcement for those who are attempting to use the management and leadership processes and to shape their skills over time.

In the meeting, no negative consequences are necessary. The natural consequence of standing before peers when you have done nothing or when you are not prepared is enough of a negative consequence. Nothing more should be forthcoming from you other than, "Thank you. Next person, please." By the way, our experience over the years is that those who have done nothing are the ones who want the most time to explain why. For this reason, make sure that you limit each presentation to three minutes. If you find that people don't have anything to present, you should realize that you have not made the work around your mission and vision positively reinforcing.

Remember that the purpose of the meeting is to give managers an opportunity to show bosses and peers their accomplishments and their process for attaining them. As the leader, you show interest in the good things the person has done by asking questions that give the person an opportunity to expound on the details and by verbally acknowledging those things that you like.

In the beginning, weekly meetings are best; but later, they can be limited to no more than monthly and ideally would be incorporated into an existing meeting. Although expectations make some people uncomfortable at first, as they see the positive nature of things, they look forward to it. This meeting also has the added advantage of promoting idea sharing and problem-solving techniques among peers during and after the meeting.

ADI worked in one of America's most admired companies, assumed to be a model for leadership development. One of the mid-level managers was generously rewarded every year for his unit's results. When we got to know this manager's employees, we learned that Ed produced 80% of the entire unit's profits. This came about because of Ed's competence, not because he had greater resources than his peers. We also learned that managers from other units regularly asked about Ed as a candidate for promotion to one of their positions. The manager always suggested that Ed was producing great results but that he was not yet quite ready to take on greater responsibility, so Ed lost many opportunities for advancement.

For the organization, this story has a sad ending. Ed left! He learned that his boss was not taking care of him and helping him grow, but was instead the reason he was stuck in a job that failed to challenge him. While Ed's boss had maximized his own bonus, the organization had experienced a loss of significant proportions.

One of the most effective leadership development models is found in multilevel marketing. If you put aside the marketing element and the fact that there are unscrupulous people in every field, you will see that the model demands that leaders recruit other leaders—they do not want order takers or subordinates. Rather they want people who want to do the same things the leader does and give them that opportunity. They use their personal relationship to build the followers' dedication to the vision and the values, encouraging them to seek more opportunities to lead others. Personal growth as a leader is measured directly by developing followers into leaders.

The test for all leaders is to keep the followers challenged. Growth comes from effort, not from success. Any weightlifter who is satisfied with lifting a certain weight will find that his muscles have stopped growing. He is now working on definition, how the muscles look rather than how they function. The serious lifters are continuously striving to lift more. The same is true of leaders. Yet, their new goal is always something they believe they can do. Goals that stretch the credulity of the follower are ridiculous. Goals that show the follower how to reach them are effective at encouraging growth.

Leadership is based on the relationship the leader has with the followers and the relationship the followers have to the leader's cause. It is incumbent on anyone desiring to be a leader to use whatever authority they have (moral, structural, or simply their personal persuasiveness) to build relationships that move toward their vision. Relationships that are relatively free of friction and that help each party experience personal benefits are the hallmarks of good leaders.

chapter 19

THE FINAL FRONTIER OF LEADERSHIP

*The final test of a leader is that he leaves behind him in others
the conviction and will to carry on.*

Walter Lippman (1945)

Self-management is a leader's greatest challenge. When you, as a leader, consider how your every action conveys a message to your followers, you realize the true burden of leadership. Every word of praise, condescension, or anger will either build or erode one's leadership legacy. Every action that a leader takes will be examined and will either inspire the followers or impair their readiness to follow. No one can be continuously conscious of his own behavior and its impact but no leader can afford to remain ignorant of how the actions and words of leaders produce a reaction in one's followers.

To develop healthy relationships with followers, leaders must have a high degree of self-awareness. Since follower behavior is a reaction to that of the leader, the leader must have clarity about his actions so that the cause-and-effect relationships can be established. This means that leaders must constantly examine their assumptions about their own actions and test those assumptions for validity. We all hold a certain number of untested and fallacious ideas about how things work. Leaders try to minimize these faulty concepts and change them as they are uncovered. Unfortunately, some ideas are pets and we want to hang onto them despite the evidence to the contrary.

We worked in a heavy manufacturing plant that had a militant unionized workforce. The repeated conflicts between the workforce and supervision produced perceptions on both sides that were not borne out by the facts. In trying to get management to deal with individual workers in a more personal and less confrontational way, we were repeatedly told that this approach would not work. We were told that the workers in this plant only wanted money and that they would only do more work if they got more money. Over the Labor Day weekend, the plant needed several workers to volunteer for overtime. At holiday pay rates, this meant from one and one-half to twice the usual pay rate for each hour worked. Of several hundred employees, there were no volunteers. Despite this evidence, management still insisted that money was the only driver their employees acknowledged. This kind of deliberate disregard for facts produced a management approach that thought of leadership as a series of successful contract negotiations.

Leaders who look inward for the explanation of follower behavior will gain a much greater appreciation for the actions of their followers. They will quickly learn that they play a substantial role in their employees' performance and that success or failure is not usually only attributed to an individual. Leaders can inspire their followers to greater successes, minimize follower initiative and success, or contribute to their failure. The self-aware leader is less likely to succumb to his press clippings and the approval of sycophants, but will stay true to the vision and values that build great organizations.

Leaders must also be aware of the influences on their own behavior. Leaders and managers tend to underestimate the ability of followers to alter leader behavior. The common concept of leadership is so closely related to control that they have difficulty thinking that the followers have a powerful impact on their own choices. Thomas Mahwinney's (2005) work shows that followers match leader reinforcement. That is, the more reinforcement the leader delivers, the more behavior the follower delivers. It also shows that when the followers' behavior no longer produces reinforcement for the leader, the leader increases his rate of punishment. Many writers have noted this phenomenon, giving it labels such as *back-up style* or *default mode of leadership*. This reciprocal nature of the relationship of leaders and their followers highlights the need for leaders to bring out the best (Daniels, 2000) in their subordinates. Successful followers produce more successful leaders.

Your behavior, then, is altered by the behavior of your followers. A leader is not completely in control, either of his/her behavior or of others' behavior. Just like everyone else, leaders respond to the consequences that the environment produces for their actions. The way to exercise some control is by engineering the environment to produce reinforcers for constructive and productive activities. The people whom one chooses to associate with are part of that environment. Their actions are either part of bringing out the best in you or they are part of bringing you to some lower level of performance and quality of life. This is why parents tell their children to choose their friends carefully. Since a leader has less ability to choose followers at work, we suggest that they receive training in how to optimize their relationships with their peers and with their leaders.

Game theory, which deals largely with how intelligent individuals interact with one another in an effort to achieve their own goals, has taught us in situation after situation that the most successful strategy is one in which we give up maximizing our own reinforcement to help others increase their level of success. The underlying behavioral principle of this theory is *contingency*. When others cooperate, so do I. When others defect, so do I. In short, we reinforce cooperation and we punish non-cooperation. We speak of this in terms of *positive accountability*. Leaders work to see that their followers get what they deserve. Since most of the followers' efforts are productive, they have earned frequent reinforcement. When merited, their inappropriate behavior must be stopped. The self-aware leader will recognize the success or failure of his followers by the frequency of his own reinforcing and punishing behaviors. The leader who punishes frequently, and is self-aware, will recognize quickly that the followers are not following. He will then take the appropriate steps to correct the situation.

We suggest that you imitate Benjamin Franklin (1997) and measure your own behavior. Franklin wanted to arrive at moral perfection. He listed 13 virtues he wished to exemplify and each week focused on one of those virtues. At the end of the day, he would examine his activities to see if he had observed or lapsed in that virtue and recorded the result in his notebook. As he noted, this practice did not enable him to reach the perfection he desired, but his improvements were real and resulted in his feeling that he had bettered himself as a result.

Our suggestion is not about your virtues but about your actions.

1. Select some behavior that you believe will produce an effective response in your followers and practice it.

2. Keep data on your actions and on the response of others.

3. Follow up on that response by others to find out if it was just a reaction to your presence or a reaction to your leadership.

4. Find out what works for you and engage in the deliberate practice of leadership.

5. Find out what does not work for you and either change it or find some way to compensate for that weakness.

6. Above all, keep data that allows you to evaluate your personal progress toward effective leadership.

It is so easy to mislead yourself when all you have is your own memory and perspective of events. Patterns of behavior often escape the casual, or the biased, observer—a circumstance that retards learning.

Leadership is not a mystery! Look around you. You will see it everywhere. If you know what to look for, you will find many good, clear examples of the best actions of leaders among your followers. You only have to know *how* to learn from your own experiences and from those of your acquaintances by analyzing those experiences from a standpoint of behavioral knowledge. In *Measure of a Leader* we sought to show you ways to demystify the concept of leadership and to give you a practical way to discover, improve, and sustain good leadership behavior. These methods, properly applied, will elevate the elusive concept into a specific and doable action.

50 THINGS YOU CAN DO TO INCREASE YOUR LEADERSHIP IMPACT

Human felicity is produced not so much by great pieces
of good fortune that seldom happen, as by little advantages that occur every day.

Benjamin Franklin (1759)

The authors have created a list of ideas to get leaders started in practicing the skills that will enhance leadership impact. All of the ideas relate to the measures proposed in Chapter 9. The list obviously contains more suggestions than leaders can comfortably use at any one time. The idea is to focus on the area of leadership that has the greatest growth potential for you.

This is also a list of suggestions leaders can use to help their followers develop their own leadership potential. You can use these items as an inventory to locate a specific skill followers need to develop. If you can use one or two of the suggestions in conjunction with the measures suggested (or similar ones), you will arrive quickly at the best way to help followers grow. And you will help followers make the connection between their behavior and that of *their* followers.

To Build Momentum (1-10)

☐　1. Get followers to teach you something. Anything!

☐　2. Find your followers' positive reinforcers.

☐　3. Verify periodically that these items or activities are still positive reinforcers for the followers.

☐　4. Measure the time from decision to action at each level of the organization.

☐　5. Ask the question, "How did you do that?" every time you learn of a result where you did not see the behaviors that generated it.

☐　6. Reinforce every behavior until the performers reach high-and-steady rates (HSR).

☐　7. Reinforce intermittently once behavior reaches HSR.

☐　8. Develop a system for discovering employees who are giving discretionary effort.

☐　9. Build reinforcement into processes and procedures.

☐　10. Arrange multiple sources of social reinforcement for your followers including reinforcement from managers, peers, customers, and suppliers.

To Build Commitment (11-26)

☐ 11. Record commitments made to customers, subordinates, bosses, and peers.

☐ 12. Track the percentage of commitments met each week.

☐ 13. Make smaller commitments.

☐ 14. Recognize all who meet their commitments.

☐ 15. Celebrate project, initiative, or program completion (or dissolution).

☐ 16. Create a vision that has emotional appeal, e.g., best in the world, number-one supplier.

☐ 17. Develop a way to visualize progress toward the vision through a scoreboard, chart, or graph.

☐ 18. Test followers to identify behaviors that support the vision.

☐ 19. Find examples of and reinforce behaviors that support the vision.

☐ 20. Celebrate the accomplishment of milestones along the way.

☐ 21. Name and define the values.

☐ 22. Teach people where the ethical boundaries are by frequently discussing far out, relevant, hypothetical examples (play "What if . . .").

☐ 23. Plan time in a scheduled meeting to collect employees' current examples of values in action.

☐ 24. Publicly recognize people who exemplify company values through some decision or action.

☐ 25. Test the organization's decisions, policies, and practices for consistency with the values.

☐ 26. Consider lack of focus as a reflection of too little reinforcement received for on-task behavior.

The following suggestions relate to how your subordinates work with their peers and with their internal and external suppliers. This is where they learn to influence those who do not report to them—a more complex set of skills. Everyone can benefit from learning the skills to produce effective interactions with people on whom they depend, but over whom they exercise no authority. Remember: leaders don't depend on position for their effectiveness.

To Build Initiative (27-39)

☐ 27. Publicly celebrate peer and supplier accomplishments.

☐ 28. Recognize high performing team members privately and get their permission to publicize their accomplishments.

☐ 29. Provide symbolic or social rewards in a memorable way.

☐ 30. Reinforce behavior; celebrate results.

☐ 31. Identify reinforcers for your peers.

☐ 32. Before making improvement changes, identify impact on internal and external customers. This will ensure that an improvement in one area is not a punisher in another area.

☐ 33. Publicize the things that one unit does to help another.

☐ 34. Reinforce people who delay their own accomplishments to help others.

☐ 35. Reinforce all improvements, no matter how small.

☐ 36. Make suggesting improvements easy.

☐ 37. Budget time and money to support the testing and development of ideas.

☐ 38. Set up reinforcers for employees who assist in testing new ideas.

☐ 39. Reward successful implementation of ideas.

The following ideas will help develop followers to be better performers. Leadership assumes competence. Followers will never become leaders if they are not perceived to be successful in their assigned responsibilities. Each leader is responsible for the success of his employees and demonstrates this best by helping them become better at their jobs.

To Build Reciprocity (40-50)

☐ 40. Set goals for a high chance of success.

☐ 41. When goals are not met, focus on making the next goals achievable, since failure makes performance more brittle and extinction more likely.

☐ 42. Make hard work rewarding by expressing your personal interest and showing enthusiasm for what people are doing.

☐ 43. Use the behaviors behind the numbers for decision making.

☐ 44. Ask others their opinions, in private and in an open forum. Act on all suggestions regardless of their significance.

☐ 45. Track the percentage of suggestions implemented and the economic impact.

☐ 46. Ask questions that allow the followers to show what they know.

☐ 47. Make some part of your direct reports' rewards contingent on their employees' successes with your initiatives.

☐ 48. Ask followers about any actions that you should start, stop, or continue.

☐ 49. Share with the followers what you are doing to improve your leadership skills.

☐ 50. Make sure that your rewards are contingent by and large on follower success.

We offer several more suggestions for teaching your followers to be leaders. Teach your employees to deal with people higher in the organization to increase their ability to effectively contribute. Teach your followers how to positively influence their leaders. Teach your followers how to take the initiative in creating a mutually reinforcing relationship with you as their leader. Followers who find ways to add value to relationships with their leaders and with others are more likely to become leaders.

REFERENCES

Abernathy, W. B. (1996). *The Sin of Wages: Where the Conventional Pay System Leads Us and How to Find a Way Out.* Atlanta: Performance Management Publications.

Barker, J. A. (1993). *Paradigms: The Business of Discovering the Future.* New York: Harper Business.

Beilock, S. L., Carr, T. H., MacMahon, C. & Starkes, J. L. (2002, March). When paying attention becomes counterproductive: Impact of divided versus skill-focused attention on novice and experienced performance of sensorimotor skills. *Journal of Experimental Psychology:* 8 (1), 6-16.

Carnegie, D. (1936). *How To Win Friends and Influence People.* New York: Simon & Schuster.

Churchill, W. (1940, June 4). Speech on Dunkirk. *House of Commons.*

Collins, J. (2001). *Good to Great.* New York: Harper Collins.

Daniels, A. C. & Daniels, J. E. (2004). *Performance Management: Changing Behavior That Drives Organizational Effectiveness (4th ed.).* Atlanta: Performance Management Publications.

Daniels, A. C. (2000). *Bringing Out the Best in People.* New York: McGraw-Hill.

Drucker, P. (1973). *Management: Tasks, Responsibilities, Practices.* New York: Harper & Row Publishers.

Dyer, G. (1963, July). Learn to say "No" to the Admiral. *U. S. Naval Institute Proceedings.* 26-35.

Eisenberger, R. (1989). *Blue Monday, The Loss of the Work Ethic in America.* New York: Paragon House.

Eisenberger, R. (1992). Learned industriousness. *Psychological Review,* 99 (2), 248-267.

Ericsson, A. et al. (1993). The role of deliberate practice in the acquisition of expert performance. *Psychological Review,* 100 (3), 363-406.

Fortune. (2004, November 29). Tough Questions for Citigroup's CEO. 114.

Franklin, B. (1997). *The Autobiography of Benjamin Franklin.* New York: Touchstone.

Gilbert, T. (1996). *Human Competence: Engineering Worthy Performance.* Amherst, MA: HRD Press.

Gladwell, M. (2005). *Blink, The Power of Thinking Without Thinking.* New York: Little, Brown and Company.

Goldratt, E. M. & Cox, J. (1999). *Theory of Constraints.* Croton-On Hudson, NY: North River Press, Inc.

Grier, J. (2000). *Nothin' But A Winner.* Nashville, TN: TowleHouse Publishing.

Heisenberg, W. (1927). *Uber du Grundprinzipien der Quantenmechanik,* FF3, no. 11, 83. Copyright 2001: David C. Cassidy.

Herrnstein, R. (1997). *The Matching Law.* Cambridge, MA: Harvard University Press.

Hinton, B. L. & Barrow J. C. (1975). The superior's reinforcing behavior as a function of reinforcements received. *Organizational Behavior and Human Performance,* 14, 123-143.

Hogan, R., Curphy, J., & Hogan, J. (1994). What we know about leadership: effectiveness and personality. *American Psychologist,* 49 (6), 493-504.

Hunt, J. W. (2001, May 11). Forget the Boss as Hero. *Financial Times.*

Kennedy, J. F. (1962, September 12). Speech at Rice University.

Komaki, J. L. (1998). *Leadership from an Operant Perspective.* London: Rutledge.

Le Monde. (2002, November 4). fr, Le maestro Charles Dutoit abdique devant la fronde de ses musicians. Available online at http://www.lemonde.fr/dh/0,5987,3238--9773241,00.html.

Lewis, M. (2003). *Moneyball.* New York: Norton.

Maremont, M. & Barnathan, J. (1995, October 23). Blind Ambition. Available online at www.businessweek.com.

Marx, J. (2005, April 20). Radar, Fairfax Digital. Available online at http://radar.smh.com.au/archives/2005/04/todays_radar_co.html.

Mawhinney, T. C. (2005). *Effective leadership in superior-subordinate diads: Theory and Data.* Unpublished study.

McLean, B. & Elkind, P. (2003). *The Smartest Guys in the Room.* New York: Portfolio Press.

Michael, J. (1982). Discriminating Between Discriminative and Motivational Functions of Stimuli. *Journal of the Experimental Analysis of Behavior,* 37, 149-155.

Michaels, E., Handfield-Jones, H. & Axelrod, B. (2001). *War for Talent.* Boston: Harvard Business School Press.

Nevin, J. A. (1988). Behavioral momentum and the partial reinforcement effect. *Psychological Bulletin,* 103 (1), 44-56.

Peter, L. J. & Hull, R. (1969). *The Peter Principle.* New York: The William Morrow Company.

Peters, T. & Waterman, R. (1982). *In Search of Excellence: Lessons from America's Best-Run Companies.* New York: HarperCollins Publishers, Inc./Warner Books.

Robinson, A. G. & Stern, S. (1997). *Corporate Creativity: How Innovation and Improvement Actually Happen.* San Francisco, CA: Berrett-Koehler Publishers, Inc.

Rosenhan, D. (1969). *The Kindness of Children.* Unpublished study.

Schofield, Major General. (1879, August 11). West Point. Address to the Corps of Cadets.

Senge, P. M. (1990). *The Fifth Discipline: The art and practice of the learning organization.* London: Random House.

Sidman, M. (1989). *Coercion and Its Fallout.* Boston, MA: Authors Cooperative, Inc.

Skinner, B. F. (1987). Whatever happened to psychology as the science of behavior? *American Psychologist,* 42 (8), 780-786.

Taylor, A. (2005, January 10). The Nine Lives of Jürgen Schrempp. *Fortune,* 92.

INDEX

ABOUT THE AUTHORS

Aubrey C. Daniels

 Dr. Aubrey C. Daniels, internationally recognized author and speaker, is the world's leading authority on behavioral science in the workplace. He founded Aubrey Daniels International in 1978 and is the author of three best-selling books widely recognized as management classics: *Bringing out the Best in People, Performance Management: Changing Behavior That Drives Organizational Effectiveness,* and *Other People's Habits.* Daniels has been featured in *The Wall Street Journal, The New York Times, The Washington Post, USA Today, Fortune, Entrepreneur, Biznet,* and by CNN, CNBC, and CBS radio. He received his undergraduate degree in psychology from Furman University and earned his master's and doctorate from the University of Florida. Daniels serves on the Board of Trustees of the Cambridge Center for Behavioral Studies and Furman University, and is an Associate of Harvard University's John F. Kennedy School of Government. His numerous awards include the Lifetime Achievement Award from the Organizational Behavior Modification Network and the Outstanding Service Award from the International Association for Behavior Analysis, which also named him a 2005 Fellow.

James E. Daniels

 James E. Daniels, vice president and senior consultant with Aubrey Daniels International, has developed productivity and quality improvement systems for corporations in the United States, Australia, Brazil, Canada, England, and Italy. A graduate of the United States Military Academy at West Point, Daniels received his master's from the University of Florida. He is a former editor of *Performance Management Magazine* and co-author of the definitive behavioral text *Performance Management: Changing Behavior that Drives Organizational Effectiveness,* 4th Edition. Daniels specializes in creating performance measurement systems for knowledge workers. He helps organizations design and implement strategies that inspire and reward the discretionary effort of employees in union and non-union environments. His clients represent a wide range of industries including (but not limited to) service, manufacturing, engineering, banking, publishing, telecommunications, nuclear power generation, travel, and sales. Daniels also applies his expertise in behavioral change techniques to enhance and ensure the effectiveness of quality improvement processes such as Six Sigma.

About ADI

Aubrey Daniels International (ADI) helps the world's leading businesses use the scientifically proven laws of human behavior to promote workplace practices vital to long-term success. By developing strategies that reinforce critical work behaviors, ADI enables clients such as Daimler Chrysler, Dollar General, and Blue Cross and Blue Shield, achieve and sustain consistently high levels of performance, building *profitable* **habits**™ within their organizations. ADI is led by Dr. Aubrey C. Daniels, the world's leading authority on behavioral science in the workplace and author of the bestselling management classic *Bringing Out the Best in People* (McGraw-Hill). Headquartered in Atlanta, the firm was founded in 1978.

Also By These Authors

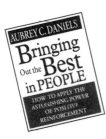

Bringing Out the Best in People

Aubrey C. Daniels

Other People's Habits

Aubrey C. Daniels

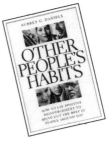

Performance Management:
Changing Behavior That Drives Organizational Effectiveness
(4ᵗʰ edition)

Aubrey C. Daniels & James E. Daniels

For more information call 1.800.223.6191
or visit our Web site www.aubreydaniels.com